LO   ACI2001

Linus Pauling

And the Chemistry of Life

Owen Gingerich
General Editor

Linus Pauling

And the Chemistry of Life

Tom Hager

Oxford University Press
New York • Oxford

Dedicated with love to Jackson, Zane, Elizabeth and, always, to Lauren

Oxford University Press

Oxford New York
Athens Auckland Bangkok Bogotá Bombay
Buenos Aires Calcutta Cape Town Dar es Salaam
Delhi Florence Hong Kong Istanbul Karachi
Kuala Lumpur Madras Madrid Melbourne
Mexico City Nairobi Paris Singapore
Taipei Tokyo Toronto Warsaw
and associated companies in
Berlin Ibadan

Copyright © 1998 by Tom Hager
Published by Oxford University Press, Inc.
198 Madison Avenue, New York, New York 10016

Design: Design Oasis
Layout: Leonard Levitsky
Picture research: Lisa Kirchner

Library of Congress Cataloging-in-Publication Data
Hager, Tom.
Linus Pauling and the chemistry of life / Tom Hager
   p. cm. — (Oxford portraits in science)
Includes bibliographic references and index.
ISBN 0-19-510853-1
1. Pauling, Linus, 1901–1994—Juvenile literature.
2. Biochemists—United States—Biography—Juvenile literature.
3. Chemists—United States—Biography—Juvenile literature.
4. Social reformers—United States—Biography—Juvenile literature.
[1. Pauling, Linus, 1901–1994. 2. Chemists.] I. Title. II. Series.
QP511.8.P37H34   1998
540'0.92—dc21
[B]   97-43403
                CIP

9 8 7 6 5 4 3 2 1

Printed in the United States of America
on acid-free paper

On the cover: *Linus Pauling in the early 1970s*; Inset: *Linus Pauling with a model of a molecule in his Caltech classroom.*
Frontispiece: *Linus Pauling in his Caltech classroom.*

Contents

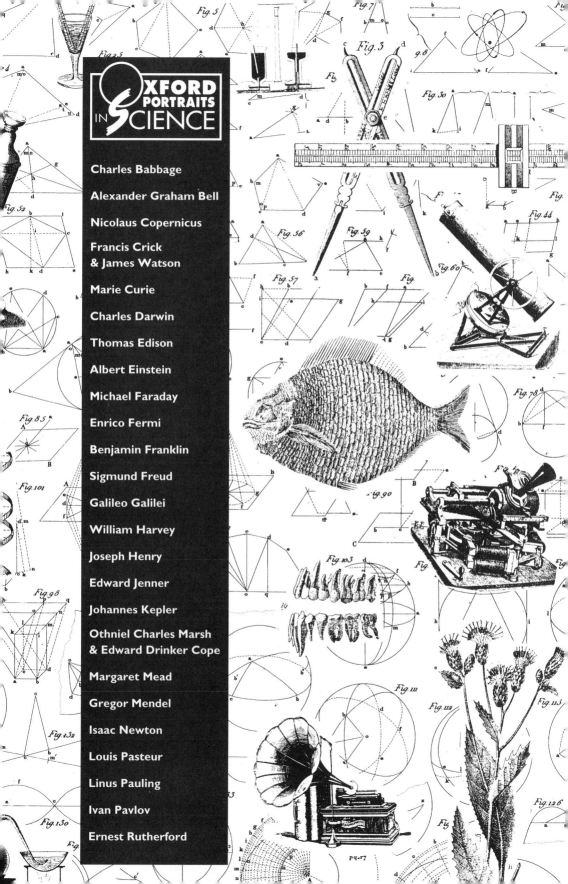

OXFORD PORTRAITS in SCIENCE

Introduction

Once, when he was 60 years old, Linus Pauling strode into a packed hall at the California Institute of Technology to deliver a guest lecture in freshman chemistry. He was followed by Jurg Waser, the class's regular teacher, loaded down with the molecular models and props Pauling liked to use in his talks. Pauling was famous for his teaching: lively and funny in front of students, fond of stunts and explosions, capable of calculating answers with six-figure precision using only a pocket slide rule, a man who filled several movable blackboards with illustrations of his points as he spoke.

Halfway through the lecture, Pauling moved aside one filled blackboard to get to a clean one behind it—and the class exploded in hoots and laughter. On the second board someone had chalked in large letters, "PAULING IS GOD, AND WASER IS HIS PROPHET." Pauling smiled, looking from the laughing students to the board. He waited until the noise died down, then picked up an eraser and wiped off "AND WASER IS HIS PROPHET," left the rest, and continued lecturing.

His students loved him. To them and many others, Linus Pauling was indeed a god of chemistry. By the time he gave the Caltech lecture, in the early 1960s, he had already described the nature of the chemical bond; pinned down the molecular structure of proteins; intuited the cause of sickle-cell anemia; engaged in the century's most famous scientific race, to determine the structure of DNA; won a

Presidential Medal of Merit for weapons research; made important discoveries in X-ray crystallography, electron diffraction, quantum mechanics, biochemistry, molecular psychiatry, nuclear physics, anesthesia, immunology, and evolution, written more than 400 articles, and created the century's most influential chemistry textbooks. He was the youngest person ever elected to the National Academy of Sciences and in 1954 had won the Nobel Prize in chemistry.

But these accomplishments were only part of his achievement. Influenced greatly by his wife, Ava Helen, Pauling had also used his scientific fame to help advance political causes, particularly the battle against the spread of nuclear weapons during the 1950s. His political activism got him into trouble, spurring a 24-year investigation by the FBI, the loss of his passport, attacks in the press, inquiries by government agencies—including threats of legal action and possible imprisonment by the U.S. Senate—and the cancellation of some of his research grants. Throughout it all, Pauling remained unmoved in his dedication to making the world a safer place. His perseverance was rewarded with a Nobel Peace Prize in 1963, making him the only person in history to win two unshared Nobels.

Pauling was a scientific giant, imaginative, bold, and unafraid of anyone and anything. He leaped over the boundaries of disciplines, from chemistry to physics to biology to medical research. He fizzed with ideas, which seemed to shoot off as fast as sparks from a pinwheel. He tied concepts and information together in ways no one had before and used his persuasive, outgoing personality to convince the world he was right. He was audacious, intuitive, stubborn, charming, irreverent, self-reliant, self-promoting—and, as it turned out, almost always correct.

Linus Pauling was the most important chemist, and arguably the most important American scientist, of the twentieth century.

And if his mother had had her way, he would have spent his life working in a machine shop.

The Boy Professor

As the train rattled toward Portland, no one took much notice of the 15-year-old who kept to himself, looking out the window at the well-tended farms and patches of black-green fir forest of Oregon's Willamette River Valley. He was thin and gawky, with a full head of auburn hair and bright blue eyes. There was nothing unusual about him— except, perhaps, the large bottle of dark liquid carefully cradled between his feet.

Inside that bottle sloshed five gallons of concentrated nitric acid. If it spilled, it would eat away the carpet and floor of the train car. It would dissolve the shoes and socks and skin on the feet of the passengers. It would get the young boy, Linus Pauling, into a great deal of trouble. But he was careful and made certain the bottle stayed upright. This was, after all, not the first time he had smuggled chemicals.

Linus was on his way home after visiting his grandparents in the little river town of Oswego, a few miles south of Portland. He treasured these visits with his father's parents, a kind couple who still spoke with strong German accents. They had taken special care of their only grandson after his

Linus Pauling stands with his mother, Belle, in 1902. Their difficult relationship helped to shape Pauling's growing sense of independence.

father died when the boy was nine years old. They had fed him treats, listened intently to his excited talk about what he had learned in school, and given him free rein to wander the countryside and go places his mother would never have let him.

Linus was something of a daredevil, who fearlessly ranged over nearby woods, creeks, and lakes and shinnied out high over the river on a train trestle. He especially enjoyed exploring the abandoned iron smelter where his grandfather worked as a night watchman. On one visit he had climbed the smelter's old smokestack, a hundred feet high, and perched there for a while enjoying the view of the river, patchwork farms, and faraway mountains.

Best of all, he found a way into the smelter's small laboratory, where iron ore had once been tested for its metal content. Although deserted for years, it was still packed with boxes of old chemicals, rusting equipment, bits and pieces of chipped glassware, and large blue bottles of acid turning dark with age.

Over the next few weeks Linus stripped the lab of everything he could carry—and even some he could not. He stuffed an old suitcase full of boxes and bottles of chemicals and carried it innocently back to his mother's boarding-house on the train. He dismantled and hauled home piecemeal a machine for distilling water. With a friend's help he dragged a complete electric furnace to a borrowed canoe, paddled it down the Willamette River, and pushed it home in a wheelbarrow two miles uphill.

Everything went into his homemade "laboratory," a basement corner he had walled off with scrap lumber. Linus had been obsessed with chemistry ever since his best friend, Lloyd Jeffress, had demonstrated some reactions with a toy chemistry set a year earlier. Linus always remembered one trick his friend had done, in which he mixed some sugar and another chemical together, added a drop of acid—and the sugar burst into flame. At the same moment, so did young Pauling's mind. "Changing substances into other substances is what impressed me," he remembered later. "In chemistry, things happen. Very striking things happen."

For Linus Pauling, having things happen, having things change, was very important. He wanted his life to change. He had been unhappy since the sudden death of his father from a perforating ulcer, a traumatic event that had thrown Linus, his mother Belle, and his two younger sisters, Pauline and Lucile, into near poverty.

This trauma involved more than money. Linus's father had been a self-taught pharmacist, a man who knew that learning was a path to success and had appreciated his young son's precocious mental abilities. At an early age, Linus had shown himself to be unusually bright and a voracious reader, racing through every book in the house, from *Alice in Wonderland* to Dante's *Inferno*. Just before his death, Linus's father wrote a letter to the editors of the local newspaper asking for suggestions for further reading for his nine-year-old son. "In order to avoid the possibility, or probability rather, of having some one advise me to have him read the Bible, I will state that it was through reading this and Darwin's theory of evolution that my son became so interested in both history and natural sciences," he explained.

But his mother did not appreciate Linus's abilities. After her husband's death, she used all her money to buy a boardinghouse and worked hard to keep her family together. But she never fully recovered from her grief. She was depressed, withdrawn, and afflicted with pernicious anemia, a chronic blood disease

Herman Pauling, Linus's father, was a self-taught pharmacist who actively encouraged Linus's budding intellect. His death, when Linus was nine, devastated the young boy.

that sapped her energy and forced her to stay in bed for days at a time.

Belle Pauling needed her children's help—Linus's especially—to keep the boardinghouse going. She needed the children to work around the house and take on outside jobs. So she could never understand why Linus preferred to be off at his grandparents', or up in his room reading, or in his laboratory. She would hector and nag, but it all seemed to go over his head. His only response was a muttered "Get to that later, Mother," or a terrible chemical odor wafting up from the basement, bothering the boarders. Linus did take odd jobs and helped as much as he felt he could. But he was distant from his mother and spent every spare minute in his basement sanctuary, alone with his thoughts and his wonderful experiments.

Using some of his father's old books, chemistry texts from the library, and ideas he picked up in his high school classes, Linus figured out for himself how to make homemade explosives: mixtures of potassium chlorate and sulfur that went off when a trolley car ran over them (the company sent a man to Linus's house to put a stop to it) and an unstable iodide of nitrogen that popped loudly when disturbed—a sort of junior-grade nitroglycerine that proved very popular at school. Acid spills ruined his pants and ate the ends off brooms. He once set fire to the wooden walls with molten phosphorus.

While he was having a very good time, he was also learning. There was a logic to chemistry, rules about what happened when you mixed one thing with another. The more rules he learned, the easier it became to make the things he wanted to. It had always been easy for Linus to remember things, and now he began to memorize, almost without knowing it, great amounts of chemistry from the books he read.

Soon he was surprising his high school teachers. His chemistry teacher, a Mr. Green, was so impressed that he allowed Linus to stay after school to help determine the heat value of the school's heating oil and coal. The school offered only one year of chemistry to its students, but Linus was so eager that Mr. Green helped him get credit for a second year of independent study.

By the time he was a senior in high school, Linus knew that he wanted to make a career in chemistry. He had read about a field called chemical engineering, where there were well-paying jobs helping industries turn the ideas of chemists into new ways to make things. He knew that a college degree was necessary to be a chemical engineer.

But going to college was not going to be easy. His mother was barely making ends meet at the boardinghouse and was constantly harping on Linus to bring in more money. He had earned cash in various ways through high school—setting pins in a bowling alley, delivering newspapers and milk and special delivery letters, even running a movie projector at a nearby theater on the weekends—and his mother assumed that when he graduated from high school he would, like most boys his age, go out and find steady work. When she heard that instead he wanted to go to college, she became furious. You do not need college, she told him. The man down at the machine shop has already offered you a fine job there. You must face up to your responsibilities and help support our family.

It was a terrible choice. Linus would either have to do what his mother asked and give up his chance for a career in chemistry, or he would have to find the strength to say no. Unsure of what to do, he turned for advice to the family of his friend Lloyd Jeffress, who had first shown him chemistry years before. Linus had spent a good deal of time at the Jeffress home, so different from his own. Lloyd's family was well educated and better off than Linus's. The Jeffress home was full of interesting books and magazines, music, and dinner-table discussions about politics and science. They recognized and appreciated Linus's chemical talents. You must go to college, they told him. During a few years of study you will not make any money, but in the end you will have a much better job with higher pay. It's the best thing not only for you but, in the long run, for your mother as well.

Heartened by their advice, Linus told his mother that, despite her wishes, he planned to enter the chemical engineering program at Oregon Agricultural College (OAC) in Corvallis, about 90 miles away. It would be inexpensive, he said, because Oregon students paid no tuition there. During the summers he could earn money for books and living expenses. At the end of four years, he told her, he would be able to find a much better job, one that would bring in more money for the family. Reluctantly, Belle gave her assent.

Linus was learning to make decisions on his own. And there would be one more challenge to authority before he left for college. Impressed by his good grades and the amount of science he was taking, OAC admitted him when he was 16 years old, early in his senior year of high school. Linus had by that time taken every science and math course he could, so he decided to leave a term early to get a head start at college. The only problem was a state rule requiring that every senior take a full year of American history. Linus figured that he could get around this by taking two terms of the class simultaneously, but the school principal refused his request. "He didn't ask me, 'What are you going to do? Are you a good student?' He just said no," Linus recalled later.

Instead of doing what his principal told him was required, Linus did what he thought was best. He left for college early—without his diploma. Linus Pauling was destined to become one of history's most famous high school dropouts.

"I will not be able, on account of my youth and inexperience, to do justice to the courses and the teaching placed before me," he confided to his diary just before coming to OAC in early 1917. He need not have worried. True, he was younger than the average freshman, but he was also brighter, especially when it concerned chemistry, and it did not take long for him to make his mark at the school. He discovered quickly that he knew as much or more about chemistry than most of his professors, none of whom had earned a Ph.D. and many of whom had only the most rudimentary knowledge of the field. With his quick mind and prodigious memory, Linus earned A's in all his science and math courses, greatly impressing his classmates. "It just seemed like all he had to do was sit down at a table, look at a book, and he'd absorb the knowledge without reading it," one remembered.

Away from his mother and the pressures of the boardinghouse, Linus began to enjoy himself. He wore the freshman beanie required of all "rooks," rooted at football

Pauling (far left) with some of the members of his fraternity at Oregon Agricultural College. His college years brought him confidence in his teaching abilities and spurred his passion for research.

games, partied at "smokers" (student boxing matches featuring heavy consumption of beer and cigars), and tried playing billiards. As a sophomore, he joined a fraternity and got a job in the chemistry department's "solution room," where he helped prepare various chemicals for laboratory use. He still had a few things to learn—on one occasion, while siphoning concentrated ammonia from a large jug, the tubing squirted enough into him to eat away the skin lining the inside of his mouth—but he mastered almost everything put before him. He even made enough money through chopping wood, mopping floors, and cutting up meat for sorority house kitchens to send some extra money home.

After his sophomore year, Linus landed the best summer job of all: testing the composition of asphalt being used to make a new system of hard-topped highways across the state. It paid well, and Linus enjoyed camping out with the road crews for weeks at a time, learning about surveying and laughing at the workers' sometimes off-color jokes. Once they gave the teenage chemist the chance to drive a steamroller and he promptly overturned it, narrowly missing killing himself. He sent all the money he earned to his mother, knowing that Belle would use what she needed and give him back the rest for college.

But as his junior year was about to begin, Linus's mother told him that she could no longer give him any of the money he had earned. Perhaps hoping that he might quit college, she told him that the needs at the boardinghouse were too great and he would have to take a year off from OAC and work.

The news confused and disheartened him, but Linus had no intention of quitting college, even if he had to delay graduation by a year. The interruption turned out better than he could have imagined, however. Learning of his problem, his chemistry professors at OAC offered him a year's contract to teach quantitative chemistry, a course to introduce students to general principles and laboratory tech-

niques that he had taken himself just the year before. Linus did not hesitate. With this job he would be able to stay on campus, keep learning chemistry, and make money at the same time.

It was a wonderful year. Linus had always been a keen critic of his own professors, noting the reasons some lectures put students to sleep while others got students as excited about chemistry as he was, and thus put a great deal of work into preparing entertaining lectures. To improve his lecturing style, he got some pointers from a professor of oratory. Linus's natural enthusiasm, his orderly, logical approach to the subject, his quick mind and hard work soon proved to students that he was not only as good as the other professors but was in many ways a decided improvement. "Lots of times the students would say, 'Well, hell, he knows more than the profs anyway,'" said one of his classmates. "He could conduct the classes better than they could." Before long they were calling him "The Boy Professor" and vying to get into his classes.

During the summer after his sophomore year of college, Pauling (second from right) took a job testing the composition of asphalt being used to make highways.

Pauling's teaching year proved important in other ways as well. He was given a staff desk in the school's small chemistry library, where between classes he could look over the newest chemical journals as they came in. He read them cover to cover, learning about the most exciting new areas of research and adding a great deal to his ever-growing mental library of chemical facts.

By the time he returned to school as a junior, he had completed his transition from a shy, unsure teenager into a self-confident, wisecracking young college man. He was never afraid to show off what he knew. One professor remembered having Linus pepper him with "embarrassing questions about the ultimate structure of matter." Teasing another, Linus wrote on a homework assignment, "I have attempted to use words of one syllable to as great an extent as practicable in order to prevent any mental strain." On one occasion a chemistry professor tried to needle him back, saying after correcting a problem, "Well now, since Linus Pauling and I get the same answer, when two great authorities agree, it must be right." Linus just looked at him innocently and asked, "Who's the other one?"

In only one area did Linus lag behind his classmates. He had trouble dating. He was critical of his looks—"The more I look at myself in the mirror, the more peculiar my physiognomy appears to me," he wrote in his diary—and had always been shy around girls. This created a problem at his fraternity, where every member was required to date every weekend. The punishment for failure was to be dunked into a bathtub full of freezing water. Pauling endured it week after week until he figured a way to get out of it. As he was being carried to the tub, he breathed very deeply, saturating his blood with oxygen. "Then I didn't struggle at all," he said. "They put me in the tub, holding me under the water, and I just lay there, lay there, lay there, and the seconds went by . . . a minute went by . . . and they pulled me out, very frightened, saying, 'He's had a heart attack or something!' Of course, I recovered, and from then on didn't have to worry about it."

Dating ceased being a problem on the first day of class in the winter term of 1922. Pauling was then teaching a chemistry course to home economics majors and stepped up to the lectern. To avoid any "boy professor" sniggering from the 25 young women facing him, he immediately asked a question. "Will you tell me all you know about ammonium hydroxide, Miss . . . " He ran his finger down the registration sheet, looking for a name he couldn't possibly mispronounce. "Miss Miller?" He looked up and into the eyes of Ava Helen Miller, a small, delicate, strikingly pretty young girl with long, dark hair. She was just 18 years old, a flirt, and, as it turned out, knew quite a bit about ammonium hydroxide.

Pauling was attracted to her almost immediately, but he held his emotions back as the days went by. Ava Helen Miller, for her part, proved to be witty, blindingly attractive, and very interested in her young professor. He must, he told himself, maintain the decorum of a proper professor–student relationship. He tried hard to appear uninterested in Ava Helen, avoiding her eyes, steering clear of her desk as he walked around the room. She responded by making him jealous, encouraging visits from other would-be beaus, who sometimes visited her by climbing through the laboratory's windows during lab sessions. Finally, Pauling passed her a note with her homework. A year or two before, he wrote, a young OAC professor had been severely criticized for the

Ava Helen Miller, seen below right in a school play, was a student in a chemistry class taught by Linus Pauling in 1922 when he was only 21 years old. The two would marry the next year.

attentions he had paid to one of his students. This was not, Pauling wrote, going to happen to him.

At the end of class, Ava Helen stormed up to his desk. "You are my chemistry instructor, so of course I expect you to teach me some chemistry," she snapped, "but I don't expect you to teach me anything else." Then she turned her back and marched off.

Undermined, Pauling's defenses crumbled. A few weeks later, Ava Helen found another note from her professor, this time asking her out for a stroll across campus. It was the beginning of a whirlwind romance. "Boys had always told me about what beautiful eyes I had or how good a dancer I was, but Linus was not overly concerned with that," Ava Helen said. "He was full of ideas and dreams. He knew what he wanted to do and it all sounded so exciting."

In the late spring, just before giving her a final grade for the class, Linus asked Ava Helen to marry him. Without hesitating, she said yes. Fully aware as always of his role as a professor, he then lowered her grade one point below what he thought it should be, in order to avoid any impression of favoritism.

WHAT HOLDS MOLECULES TOGETHER?

When Linus Pauling was in college, all chemists knew that atoms came in distinct sizes, each called an element. Atoms in turn combined with others in simple whole-number proportions to form larger molecules: two hydrogen atoms and one oxygen atom joined to form water, and so forth. Each element preferred to make a specific number of links to others—carbon preferred making four bonds to other atoms, hydrogen only one, for instance—a combining ability known as the element's valence.

But no one knew why elements combined in just these proportions, or what forces held them together. Whoever solved that mystery would hold the key to making sense of much of chemistry.

During his year of teaching at OAC, Pauling read one attempt at an answer in the papers of Gilbert Newton Lewis, the head of chemistry at the University of California at Berkeley, and Irving Langmuir, a General Electric company chemist who would later become the first industrial chemist to win the Nobel Prize. They believed that an element's valence arose naturally from its structure.

Just a few years before, the British physicist Ernest Rutherford had shown that atoms were made of incredibly dense, positively charged nuclei surrounded by a number of smaller, negatively charged electrons. Each element was distinguished by its own specific number of electrons. Lewis and Langmuir compared those numbers to the periodic table of the elements and concluded that atoms were most stable when they were surrounded by shells that contained eight electrons at a time (except for the innermost shell, which was stable with two electrons). If an atom had only seven electrons in its outer shell, it would tend to build a stable eight-electron structure by combining with another atom that had an extra electron. The result would be a "shared electron" chemical bond between the two atoms.

Pauling was fascinated by this idea. He had learned, and was teaching his students, the old "hook and eye" theory of chemical bonding, in which certain elements were said to have a certain number of "hooks" and others a given number of "eyes." This way of explaining why elements combined with others in certain proportions really explained nothing. But Lewis and Langmuir, with their model based on the most recent ideas about atomic structure, seemed to be on to something important.

Witness to Revolution

Linus Pauling did more at Oregon Agricultural College than learn science and fall in love. He began to build a strong sense of self-confidence, a belief in his abilities to teach and to think critically. And he enlarged his understanding of society. His ceaseless reading included the stories of the French writer Guy de Maupassant, with their lessons about human nature, and the plays of the British social critic George Bernard Shaw, whose wit and insight started him thinking about the many ways in which a society built around privileged classes and private wealth could hurt its poorer and less fortunate members.

Most important, Ava Helen spurred his thinking about the issues of the day. She came from a politically active, left-wing family. Like Shaw, she was attracted to a political system called socialism. Socialists believed that the fairest society was not one in which a few wealthy people owned the means of making and distributing goods—the system in place in the United States and many other nations—but one in which all the people, rich and poor, shared ownership of the factories and railroads, shipping lines and newspapers. Ava Helen grew up amid long discussions about

Linus Pauling in 1925, after receiving his Ph.D. from Caltech. He would spend most of the next two years in Europe, learning the revolutionary new ideas of quantum physics.

women's rights and the wrongs of the American economic system. Pauling, although he was more interested in chemistry than anything else, began listening to Ava Helen's ideas, too.

Linus Pauling was learning to become more than a single-minded scientist. Slowly he began developing an interest in human affairs and science's role in society. At his OAC graduation ceremony, in the spring of 1922, he gave the senior oration, a formal speech in which he hinted at his expanding concerns.

"Advancement and growth depend upon the discovery and development of the resources of nature, and the investigation and interpretation of the laws of nature," he told the crowd of parents, professors, and students. "In the course of progress social relations are strained, and industrial, political and educational problems arise. The country is crying for a solution of all these difficulties, and is hopefully looking to the educated man for it. This, then, is the way we can repay OAC—by service . . . service to our fellow men."

This growing moral sense helped push Pauling away from his original goal of becoming an industrial chemical engineer and toward science at a higher level. He wanted to teach and do important original research that would make a significant difference in the history of chemistry. He wanted to be a university professor.

To reach that goal, he knew that he would need a doctoral degree, so he applied to a number of graduate schools during his senior year. Many accepted him, including Harvard, the University of Illinois, and the University of California at Berkeley. But a combination of haste and need led him to say yes to the school that responded most quickly with the most generous offer of support: the California Institute of Technology.

Caltech, as students called it, was a gamble for Pauling. It was a very young school with a small campus in Pasadena. It was not yet as well known as the other programs he had applied to. But Caltech had something the other schools did not.

Caltech had Arthur Amos Noyes, an internationally known chemical theorist, a money-making inventor, the author of widely used textbooks, and a great teacher. Noyes had become something of a legend by transforming the chemistry department at the Massachusetts Institute of Technology into the envy of the world. He then had been lured to Caltech by the offer of a great deal of money, a new laboratory building, and a free hand in developing the school's curriculum.

Noyes arrived full-time in 1919, bringing with him his stellar reputation, a gentle manner, and a commitment to build a school where science would be taught in a new way. Noyes believed deeply that all the sciences should learn from one another, a lesson he had learned from his own master, a great German chemist named Wilhelm Ostwald. Ostwald had moved chemistry forward by infusing it with the techniques and mathematical approach of physics, help-ing to create a new field called physical chemistry. At Caltech, Noyes made certain that chemistry students also learned everything possible about physics, mathematics, biology, and the humanities, whenever possible in small seminars that emphasized the latest research findings. He encouraged an atmosphere in which students and professors regularly interacted, formally and informally, whether in laboratories or on camping trips. He would make Caltech, as he had MIT, a renowned center for the study of chem-istry, a sort of chemical Camelot that drew the best researchers and teachers. In turn, Noyes's students gave him the appropriate and affectionate nickname of King Arthur.

Pauling knew of King Arthur and was thus flattered when Noyes wrote him personally the summer after his graduation from OAC, asking questions about his academic background, sending him the galley proofs of a new text-book he was writing, and asking Pauling to solve the 500 test questions at the ends of the chapters. Pauling worked on the questions in the summer evenings after graduation. "I learned a great deal about physical chemistry during the three months of the summer," Pauling remembered. He solved every one of Noyes's problems—and impressed King Arthur by suggesting improvements in his text.

When Pauling boarded the southbound train to Pasadena at the end of the summer of 1922, Ava Helen was not with him. The news of their engagement had come as an unpleasant shock to both of their mothers. Belle Pauling felt her son was too young to marry and would be unable to support his wife on a graduate student's stipend. Ava Helen's mother thought her daughter was throwing away her chance for a college degree. Both strongly advised their offspring to put off marriage. Reluctantly, the young lovers agreed.

Though Pauling missed Ava Helen deeply, he was also caught up in the excitement of moving to a new place. He had never been to California, and he found that he liked Pasadena—a small, wealthy bedroom community of Los Angeles—a great deal. The climate was Mediterranean, the colors pastel, the sun warm, the air soft. There were palm trees and orange groves. It was a welcome change from the dark winters, gray-green fir forests, and chilling rains of Oregon.

Pauling threw himself into his studies. During his first year at Caltech, he remembered, "I had, I think, 45 hours (which at some universities would be called 15 hours) of classwork. Later on, the department made a rule that a teaching fellow could only sign up for 30 hours. In addition, I spent a lot of time on research. After dinner, I would go back to the lab and work until perhaps 11 o'clock at night. On Saturday and Sunday, I'd just work all day."

In order to save money, Pauling shared a bed with Paul Emmett, an OAC friend who was also attending Caltech. They used it in sequence, with Emmett sleeping until

Pauling returned from the laboratory and finished writing his daily letter to Ava Helen at around three o'clock in the morning, then Pauling turning in while Emmett got up to study.

It was hard work and the hours were long—and Pauling loved it. He found that Caltech, new as it was—there were only 10 graduate students in chemistry—was a great place to learn science. Pauling had taken a great deal of chemistry while at OAC, but very little mathematics or physics. Now he made up for this deficiency by learning advanced calculus, vector analysis, integral equations, complex numbers and potential theory, classical physics and quantum theory, advanced physical chemistry, and atomic spectroscopy. He attended weekly seminars in astronomy and physics that often featured visiting scientists and leading researchers from around the world. From them he learned of the very latest and most exciting scientific advances, sometimes even before they were published.

Pauling (front row, far left) poses with the faculty and staff of Caltech's chemistry department in 1923. As a graduate student, Pauling impressed his Caltech professors by mastering both laboratory research and theoretical inquiry.

Intellectually, Pauling had never been happier. Emotionally, things were not going as well. As time went by and a date for their wedding seemed to come no closer, the tone of Ava Helen's daily letters shifted toward the accusatory; she wrote that she thought Pauling was delaying their marriage to satisfy his personal ambitions. He replied that he had agreed to put off the marriage only in order to be better able to support her, writing that "your happiness means everything to me, dear heart, when my heart is so full of love for you."

To keep her happy, Pauling agreed within months of starting at Caltech that they would get married the following summer. During the school year, he bought a used Model T Ford from a professor for $50 and learned to drive it by taking it around the block a few times. As soon as his first year was over he headed north to Oregon. In June 1923 he and Ava Helen were married in a small family ceremony at her sister's house in Salem. After a one-day honeymoon, Pauling started another summer job of testing pavement for Oregon road crews. But this time he had a young bride with him.

It was a euphoric summer. The Paulings moved from town to town with the road crew, staying in cheap hotel rooms and shabby apartments up and down the Columbia River. They learned everything about each other—some of it, from Pauling's standpoint, surprising. One weekend Pauling checked out a book on intelligence tests from a local library, and he and Ava Helen began answering the questions together. "Much to my astonishment," he said, "I found that my newly acquired wife could work these mathematical problems faster than I could, and get the right answer more often than I could." More important, they both learned that they had found true soulmates, equals intellectually as well as emotionally. Theirs would be a deep, lifelong love.

In the fall, the young couple took up residence in a modest house near Caltech. They did not have much money to live on, but Ava Helen proved adept at stretching what they had. She became an accomplished cook and spent time keeping the tiny house clean. But she was too bright and spirited to be a stay-at-home wife. The all-male faculty and student body of Caltech were amused to see her accompanying her husband to occasional classes during the day. In the evenings, they were always together in the laboratory, where she helped him make measurements, draw diagrams, calculate figures, and keep his laboratory notes. Ava Helen would never be relegated to the role of a traditional wife. She was determined to be more than a background figure who ran the house while her husband worked.

Graduate students in chemistry are expected not only to learn in the classroom but to prove that they can make discoveries in the laboratory. This part of their training is done in the laboratories of major professors who guide their work, teaching them both how to handle equipment and how to conceive experiments that will answer important questions. Pauling's major professor, Noyes decided, would be Roscoe Dickinson, a young professor who served as Caltech's resident expert in an exciting new technique that would become Pauling's most important scientific tool.

This procedure was called X-ray crystallography, and the way it worked was almost magical. Almost all solids exist in crystalline forms, in which the atoms are arranged in repeating three-dimensional patterns. Some crystals, including those in many metals, are too small to see with the naked eye. Others, such as rock salt or quartz, can grow very large. In 1912, a German physicist discovered that by shooting a beam of X rays at crystals and then analyzing the way the X rays scattered—their "diffraction pattern"— researchers could painstakingly work out, at least for simple crystals, the distances and angles between the atoms that comprised them.

This seemed incredible. The finest microscopes of the day could barely make out the bits and pieces inside living cells, but in one leap X-ray crystallography made it possible to pin down the positions of atoms 10,000 times smaller. It was true that the technique could be used only for very simple crystal structures—those with more than six or eight atoms in their repeating units gave diffraction patterns too complex to analyze—but even so, X-ray crystallography was beginning to do for the study of chemicals what Galileo's discovery of the telescope did for astronomy: change things forever. The structure of molecules, the way atoms joined together to build them, had been guessed at for decades. But without any way to verify these guesses, structural studies had thus far been deemed by most chemists to be a waste of time.

As Pauling took up the technique, only 10 years after its discovery, laboratories in Europe were already describing the atomic architecture of dozens of crystals, from rock salt to diamonds. They were confirming some old theories—finding, as predicted, that carbon atoms often join to make three-sided pyramids called tetrahedra—but throwing out others. Hard data about structure at the atomic level could now, for the first time in human history, be used to test chemists' ideas.

Under Roscoe Dickinson's guidance, Pauling learned how to use the finicky and complicated X-ray instrument, how to grow his own crystals, how to cut and polish them at specific angles, place them carefully in the apparatus, capture the X-ray diffraction patterns on photographic plates, measure the intensity and position of each important point, and analyze the patterns mathematically to see what they said about the atomic structure.

It was very hard work, with several things that could go wrong at each step, and at first Pauling experienced nothing but frustration. He spent three weeks trying to piece together the structure of one crystal, only to learn from a journal article that a Dutch team had beaten him to it. Again and again he took a preliminary look at different crystals, only to find that their structures were too complex to be analyzed.

After two months of frustration working with 15 different substances, Dickinson rescued him. The professor took him to the chemistry stockroom, grabbed a piece of molybdenite—a shiny black crystalline mineral composed of sulfur and molybdenum—showed him an innovative way of preparing it in thin slices, and helped him take the X-ray photographs.

Within a month, Pauling and Dickinson had pinned down its atomic structure. Molybdenite turned out to be moderately surprising, the first substance ever described in which six atoms of a nonmetal, sulfur, were arrayed in an equal-sided prism around a metal atom, molybdenum.

Pauling was elated. This was his first success in the laboratory, his first real discovery. "I was pleased to learn that questions about the nature of the world could be answered by carefully planned and executed experiments," he later wrote. The analysis of molybdenum's structure opened the door. He followed it by discovering the atomic structures of four more crystals over the next two years—a sparkling record of achievement for a graduate student.

But laboratory work would never be his first love. It was difficult for Pauling to slow his restless mind and find the patience needed for meticulous, repeated experiments. He loved coming up with new ideas and would most often, in later years, let someone else gather the experimental proof.

There was no doubt after his first months at Caltech that Pauling was doing well, and Noyes was pleased to see it. By Pauling's second year, Noyes was showing him special favor, asking Pauling's advice and introducing him to important visiting scientists. Thanks to Noyes's encouragement, Pauling, while still a graduate student, expanded his scientific work beyond the laboratory, cowriting theoretical papers with Peter Debye, an international leader in physical chemistry who was visiting Caltech, and Richard Tolman, a respected member of the school's chemistry division.

A wide scientific world was opening before Pauling, and he was interested in almost all of it, from the makeup of atoms to the structure of dwarf stars. But increasingly, one question began to stand out from among all the others.

It arose from the connections Pauling was making between the *structure* of molecules—the distances and angles between the atoms that comprised them—and their *behavior*, their melting and boiling points, the energy required to break them apart and re-form them.

Pauling believed that the two characteristics were intimately entwined. A full understanding of molecular structure, he thought, could explain a great deal—perhaps everything—about chemical behavior.

What was needed was a new way of understanding molecular structure from the bottom up, from the basic laws of nature. What determined structure? What dictated why atoms arranged themselves in certain ways but not others? What made the bonds between some atoms very strong and others weak? Underlying laws certainly determined these properties—rules of the sort that Pauling had read about in the papers of Gilbert Newton Lewis and Irving Langmuir— but Lewis and Langmuir had not gone far enough.

Pauling wanted to take the next step. At Caltech, in his many physics classes, he realized that in order to unravel the secret of molecular structure he would have to understand the nature of the atoms that made up the molecules, just as an architect who wants to make buildings has to know a great deal about the strength and capabilities of beams, bricks, and boards. Immersing himself in physics, Pauling began learning everything he could about the fast-changing theories of atomic structure. Things in this field were changing almost weekly as new findings came in from Europe, where a revolution in physics was taking place. A small group of young theorists had declared war on the idea of the atom as a miniature solar system, with electrons zipping around the nucleus. This model left too many questions unanswered, they said, including why it was that the negatively charged electrons did not lose energy, as the laws of physics said they should, and fall into the positively charged nucleus. All of the debate was cloaked in difficult mathematics, and Pauling worked hard at Caltech to understand these new ideas. Then the Paulings' lives were changed in another way. In March 1925, Ava Helen gave birth to a son, Linus, Jr. It was a joyful event in many ways, but stressful in others. Intent on his work, Pauling did not change his schedule, continuing to labor late in the laboratory even after he received his doctoral degree, with honors, in June. But Ava Helen's life was transformed. The new baby meant she could no longer be her husband's laboratory mate. She now spent most of her days at home, washing, cleaning, and caring for the infant.

Just after Linus, Jr., was born, Pauling learned that he had won a Guggenheim Fellowship to study the new physics in Europe. He assumed that the baby would come along and was "shocked," he later said, when Ava Helen suggested leaving him with her mother until they returned. She pointed out the difficulty of traveling long distances with a baby in tow, with little time for dealing with the infant's needs and limited money for babysitters. After thinking it over, Pauling agreed. They would be apart from their baby for more than a year. There were good reasons for it, but their first European trip set a pattern: For Pauling, science and

The birth of the Paulings' first son, Linus, Jr., in 1926 came just as Linus learned that he had won a fellowship to study in Europe. The new baby was left in the care of Ava Helen's mother for more than a year while the young couple was overseas.

Ava Helen came first. His children would always place a distant third.

They arrived in Naples in the spring of 1926 and for several weeks enjoyed the honeymoon they had never really had, touring Rome and Florence, being jostled by the crowds in front of St. Peter's, and admiring the ruins at Paestum. It was glorious.

But Pauling was eager to get to work. He had arranged to study with Arnold Sommerfeld, one of the world's leading physicists, whose institute at the University of Munich was a nerve center for the development of new ideas about atomic structure. Short and slight, but still a commanding figure with his waxed mustache and dueling scar, Sommerfeld had a knack for turning out the brightest scientific minds in Europe. He knew everyone in theoretical physics, had collaborated on solving problems with the greatest of them, loved talking about the latest ideas with his students, and was a terrific teacher. Everyone who was anyone in physics corresponded with Sommerfeld, and he used the letters and prepublication papers that came to him from all the leaders in the field as fodder for his students.

When Pauling arrived, the institute was abuzz with a radically new approach to understanding the atom that had been proposed by one of Sommerfeld's former students, Werner Heisenberg. This young firebrand had decided to throw out any visualizable ideas of the atom at all and work instead with pure mathematics to explain the way atoms behaved. He came up with a system called matrix mechanics that was very difficult to use but provided answers that matched reality. His work was causing a furor among traditional physicists, who thought it absurd to form a theory without a physical picture of the atom behind it.

Then, just as the Paulings were settling into a tiny apartment a few blocks from the University of Munich, another, seemingly very different, theory was presented by one of Heisenberg's critics, the Austrian physicist Erwin

Schrödinger. In Schrödinger's view, electrons behaved not like tiny circling planets but like waves surrounding the nucleus. By applying the mathematics of wave functions, Schrödinger was able to create equations that also matched the observed properties of simple atoms.

Pauling heard firsthand the sometimes acrimonious debate between adherents of Heisenberg's matrices and Schrödinger's waves. In the summer of 1926 he saw Schrödinger present his wave ideas for the first time in Munich where the young Heisenberg jumped up at the end of the lecture to challenge his views. For a while it looked as though the physics world might split into two warring camps. But over the months Pauling was in Europe, it began to become clear that Schrödinger's and Heisenberg's ideas were not different realities but two different mathematical methods for arriving at the same atomic reality. Ultimately they became joined under a new name: quantum mechanics. Researchers, it seemed, could pick whichever method was easiest to use for a particular problem.

Pauling came to prefer Schrödinger's wave approach. "I find his methods much simpler than matrix calculations; and the fundamental ideas more satisfactory," he wrote a friend from Munich, "for there is at least a trace of physical picture behind the mathematics."

He then took Schrödinger's ideas to the next step. If electrons acted like waves, then what happened when two atoms joined together? Did the waves combine completely and now surround both of the nuclei? Or did the waves simply overlap a little? Pauling spent many nights in Munich working on this question, trying to tame Schrödinger's formidable equations and make them work to explain the bonds between atoms.

There was time for fun as well, however. Pauling had taken German in college and could now conduct passable conversations with the students, professors, and shopkeepers around him. He and Ava Helen went to the opera and

text continues on page 40

BOHR'S ATOM

While Pauling was at Caltech, a small group of European theorists led by Niels Bohr was rethinking how the world is made. Bohr's ideas seemed, at first, bizarre. He believed in the theories of Max Planck, a German physicist who in 1901 had proposed that forms of energy such as heat and light were not continuous and smooth, as Newton had thought, but grainy and discontinuous, made of discrete bits he called quanta. Evidence in favor of Planck's quanta grew throughout the first decade of the 20th century until 1913 when Bohr, then 28 years old, proposed that the atom itself was a quantum system.

In Bohr's theory, the atom consisted of electrons circling the nucleus, but only at specific distances from the nucleus, orbits with diameters restricted by quantum rules. Add a quantum of energy to the atom and a Bohr electron would "jump" from an orbit closer to the nucleus to one farther away. Then, falling back to a more stable orbit, it would release a quantum of energy, sometimes in the form of visible light.

Bohr's theory offered an explanation of why elements gave off characteristic wavelengths of light when they were heated, patterns of light that could be passed through a prism and studied, and which formed a sort of spectral fingerprint for each element. Because each element had its own unique set of electrons, each when heated would be expected to throw off a distinctive pattern of light as the electrons fell back into their original orbits.

By the early 1920s, Bohr, refining his ideas through work with the German physicist Arnold Sommerfeld, was drawing pictures of atoms that looked like gorgeous geometric flowers, their intricate petaling formed of elongated, elliptical, interpenetrating electron orbits that were all carefully related to the elements' spectral patterns. During the years Pauling was at Caltech, those complex atomic constructions, with their pulsing, wheeling, harmonious electron orbit and chordlike sets of light-lines, appeared to represent, as Sommerfeld said, "the true music of the spheres."

But there were still questions. How could electrons disappear from one orbit and reappear in another without existing anywhere in between, having

European physicists Arnold Sommerfeld (left) and Niels Bohr were among those who revolutionized physics during the 1920s by refounding it on new ideas about the structure and behavior of atoms.

made the "quantum leap" Bohr's model demanded, one that was deemed impossible by classical physics? And how could negatively charged electrons circle a positively charged nucleus without losing energy, as classical physics demanded of moving, charged bodies? Bohr's work raised almost as many questions as it answered. While the old, classical physics did not seem to work at the level of the atom, neither, in the mid-1920s, did Bohr's. During the time Pauling was studying the field at Caltech, "It looked for a while," as one contemporary observer wrote, "as though either the physicists or physics itself had become completely insane."

It would take a new synthesis called quantum mechanics to solve the conundrum.

text continued from page 37

visited galleries. They toured the new Deutsches Museum, with its extensive scientific exhibits, joined other students for hiking trips to the nearby Alps, and sometimes went dancing at Odeon's Casino. "I love to dance with Linus for he is such a good dancer," Ava Helen wrote in a letter home that summer. "We get along wonderfully well and do lots of little steps that other people can't do."

The only dark period came in July 1926, when Pauling received a letter from his sister Lucile saying that their mother had died. Although only 45 years old, Belle had grown increasingly frail after Pauling left for Europe, her pernicious anemia sapping her strength and causing her to have delusions. She had died, his sister wrote, in a state hospital psychiatric ward. Pauling wept as he read it.

But he buried what grief he had in work. Sommerfeld was teaching him the mathematics he needed to succeed with Schrödinger's wave equation, and he began applying this method successfully to problems. A great breakthrough came when he used wave mechanics to explain some of the basic properties, including the size, of large atoms with many electrons. This important step forward won him Sommerfeld's admiration and publication in the prestigious British journal *Proceedings of the Royal Society*. He next figured out how to use the new physics to predict the sizes of atoms as they existed in crystals.

These were noteworthy advances, but they still did not address Pauling's driving question about the bonds between atoms. Applying Schrödinger's mathematics to complexes of more than one atom simply did not seem to work, and Sommerfeld was not able to help him. In February 1927 he and Ava Helen left Munich to search for answers elsewhere. They first traveled to Copenhagen, where Pauling failed to catch the attention of the great Danish quantum physicist Niels Bohr. The next stop was Zurich, where he was unsuccessful in his attempts to work with Schrödinger as well. "I have rather regretted the nearly two months spent

A page from Pauling's 1927 article in The Proceedings of the Royal Society, *in which he pioneered the use of quantum mechanics to predict the size and other properties of atoms. This paper marked Pauling's debut on the international scientific stage.*

186   L. Pauling.

It will be observed that the function differs appreciably from zero only within a radius of the order of magnitude of the major axis of the corresponding ellipses of the old quantum theory ; namely, $r = 2a_0n^2/Z$, or $\xi = 4n$, as was remarked by Schrödinger (I). In fig. 2 are given values of D as a function of

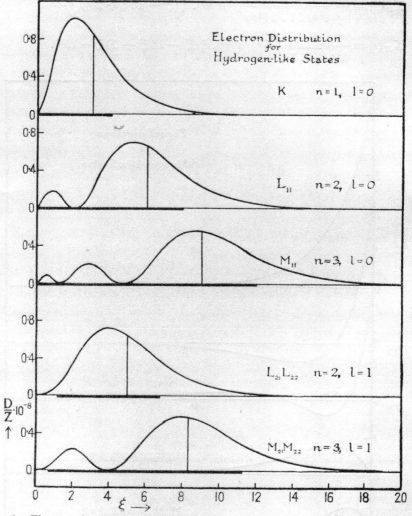

FIG. 2.—Electron distribution for hydrogen-like states ; the ordinates are values of $D \cdot Z^{-1} \cdot 10^{-8}$, in which $D = 4\pi r^2 \rho$, with ρ the electron density. The vertical lines correspond to $\bar{r}$, the average value of r.

here," Pauling wrote a friend from Zurich in August 1927, "for I have been unable to get in touch with Schrödinger. I saw him about once a week, at a seminar. I tried very hard to find out what he is doing, and I offered to make any calculations interesting to him since he was not interested in my work; but without success."

Even worse, Pauling found out in Zurich that he would not be the first to apply wave mechanics to the chemical bond. Two young German acquaintances of his, Walter Heitler and Fritz London, had beaten him to it. Working closely with Schrödinger, they had found a way to use the wave equation to create a mathematical model of a simple chemical bond.

Their breakthrough was made possible by a new idea of Heisenberg's called exchange energy. This theory proposed that as two atoms approached each other the chances would increase that a negatively charged electron from one would find itself attracted to the positively charged nucleus of the other, and the same thing would happen from the other side. At a certain point, the two electrons would begin jumping back and forth between the two nuclei, creating an electron exchange that would happen billions of times per second. In a sense, the two electrons would no longer be able to tell which nucleus they belonged to.

Combining this idea with Schrödinger's wave equation, Heitler and London calculated that the attractive energy of this electron exchange would be balanced at a certain point by the repulsion of the two positively charged nuclei, creating a chemical bond with a definite length and strength. They proved their point by calculating the bond between two hydrogen atoms.

It was a great triumph, the first extension of Schrödinger's wave mechanics to the level of molecules and the first time the new physics had been used successfully to explain the nature of chemical bonds. Pauling scrutinized Heitler and London's results while he was in Zurich and talked with them often. He became convinced that they were right and recognized that his own efforts had failed because he had not used the essential idea of the electron exchange.

But there was a great deal left to do. Heitler's and London's work was just a first step. They had worked out only the simplest hydrogen molecule. There were many more problems to be solved with this new approach. Pauling determined that he would be the one to solve them.

3

The Bond

Caltech was booming when the Paulings returned from their European stay in the fall of 1927. The number of students at the school had grown to 600, including 100 graduate students. Departments of geology and biology had been started. An aeronautics laboratory was on the drawing board. Funds were being raised to build the world's largest telescope, on nearby Mount Wilson. A steady stream of respected scientific visitors, including Werner Heisenberg, Arnold Sommerfeld, and Albert Einstein, kept professors and students abreast of the latest scientific findings. And more-than-adequate research funding, from both private donors and philanthropic foundations, was assured by the presence of Arthur Noyes and the Institute's leader, Nobel Prize–winning physicist Robert Millikan.

It was an exciting place to be for the new, 26-year-old assistant professor of theoretical chemistry, Linus Pauling. He was thrilled to have his first official office (a corner of the X-ray laboratory), his first graduate student (a Texan, J. Holmes Sturdivant, who quickly became a lifelong friend), and his first class to teach ("An Introduction to Wave Mechanics with Applications to Chemistry"). He was

proud to be an academic colleague of the men who had taught him just two years earlier.

And Pauling quickly proved his abilities. In the classroom, he became known as an exciting and stimulating teacher, as well as a leading expositor of the newest ideas in quantum physics. But his real proving ground would be research. Pauling's former professor, Roscoe Dickinson, put him in charge of running the X-ray crystallography program, where he set Sturdivant to work solving new crystal structures. Pauling finished cowriting a book about spectroscopy with Samuel Goudsmit, a young Dutch doctoral student he had met in Europe. He wrote a long scientific article that introduced American chemists to the

Heitler-London approach to the chemical bond—and added some new ideas of his own.

Pauling worked hard to extend Heitler and London's ideas to more complex molecules. But he was immediately faced with a mathematical roadblock. Heitler and London's approach depended on applying Schrödinger's difficult wave equation to every electron in a molecule—a daunting process even for the interaction of two simple atoms that quickly became impossible for the interaction of more complex atoms.

While he was working on this problem, another one caught his attention. X-ray crystallography was impossible to use on any but the simplest chemical structures, because anything more involved produced complicated X-ray diffraction patterns far too intricate to decode in the days before computers.

In both cases, Pauling needed to find approximations and shortcuts to help with the difficult mathematics. And here he discovered a talent that would be a key to his success as a scientist: He was very good at simplifying things.

Pauling's unusually powerful memory enabled him to store vast amounts of information, to build huge mental libraries of facts from chemistry, X-ray crystallography, mathematics, and physics. Rather than getting lost in the piles of facts and figures he had memorized, Pauling had the ability to focus on a particular problem and pull out the information relevant to it—rather like today's computer database programs, which, given the right keywords to search for, can sift through enormous amounts of information and pull out needed records.

Access to information was not enough by itself, however. The gathered facts also had to be put together in the right way to form an answer. In 1928, Pauling applied himself to solving the complicated structures of an important family of minerals called the silicates, which include topaz, talc, and mica. He knew it was likely that these minerals were composed of basic repeating units that included dozens of atoms, far too large a problem to solve directly with X-ray crystallography. So he began working at it the other way, from the bottom up, by thinking not about the whole daunting structure at once but breaking it down into basic pieces.

Pauling knew which atoms were involved. Silicates were made mostly of silicon and oxygen with a sprinkling of metal atoms. In England, one of the pioneers of X-ray crystallography, William Lawrence Bragg, had also been studying the silicates. Bragg thought of the atoms in silicates as though they were different-sized marbles in a box, with oxygen and silicon rather large, the metal atoms much smaller. The basic silicate structure, Bragg thought, would be determined by the ways the larger marbles fit together, the smaller ones could then be tucked between.

Pauling read Bragg's work and thought very highly of it. But he also understood that Bragg, a physicist, was missing something important. Chemists like Pauling thought of atoms not as separate marbles that could arrange themselves any which way but as elements that bound themselves to other elements in specific ratios.

Silicon, Pauling knew, was similar to carbon in many ways, including in its ability to bind to other atoms. Chemists call an atom's binding ability its valence. Both carbon and silicon have a basic valence of four—that is, they are most likely to bind in a stable manner to four other atoms at a time. Pauling knew as well that when carbon bound to four other atoms it did so in a way that formed a four-sided pyramid called a tetrahedron, with the carbon atom in the middle and the points at the top and the base of the pyramid being formed by the other four atoms. There was evidence that silicon formed the same shape.

Pauling also knew that oxygen atoms in crystals often formed an octahedron, a cube-shaped arrangement, with other elements. Instead of marbles in a box, Pauling began thinking of pyramids and cubes. With these basic shapes in mind, he thought next about how the blocks fit together and what determined whether they shared a side or only a point or an entire face. He began doodling pictures and then, with Ava Helen's help, started folding the three-dimensional shapes out of paper and sewing them together. These paper models helped him tremendously: He could now see what fit and what did not, and try new combinations again and again.

He made his models according to a specific set of rules. The sizes of the atoms and ions involved had to match known values; the lengths and positions of bonds between ions had to correlate reasonably with what was already known from the X-ray crystallography of simpler molecules; and the positive and negative electrical charges of neighboring ions had to balance out. To these he added more rules that he discovered himself about how many blocks could fit at a corner or along an edge.

This proved something like a game. By playing the game fairly, with his imagination reined in tightly by the chemical rules he already knew about, Pauling found he could build theoretical models of silicates that seemed to match the complicated X-ray data. This was a process of working backwards, of course—modeling something likely to produce an X-ray pattern rather than using the X-ray pattern to determine a model—but by doing it in strict conformity to what was known of chemistry and physics, and abiding by the reasonable rules he had created, he found that he could come up with structures that seemed logical and, in fact, seemed to be the only ones possible.

It turned out Pauling was right. His combination of rule making and model building allowed him to crack the structures of mica, talc, topaz, and other seemingly unsolvable minerals. The publication in 1928 of Pauling's guidelines for solving the silicates and other ionic crystals marked his first great international scientific triumph. Pauling's

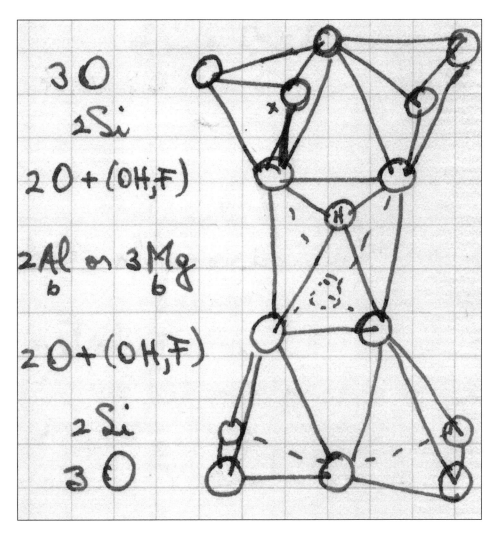

Rules, as they became known, simplified a complicated field, showed other researchers a new way to solve more complex crystal structures, and made Pauling at age 27 famous among crystallographers. Lawrence Bragg himself credited Pauling with developing "the cardinal principle of mineral chemistry."

This was a wonderful step forward for Pauling's career, one that might have been enough to satisfy many young chemists. But it was not enough for Pauling. He now threw himself totally into extending Heitler and London's concept

This sketch from Pauling's research notes shows a proposed structure for a silicate crystal—the type of complex molecular structure impossible to solve before Pauling developed a new approach.

of the chemical bond to all of chemistry. Pauling hammered away at the problem, but for more than two years the answers eluded him. His mind, too restless to stay on any one problem for too long, wandered to other questions. He solved more crystal structures and published an important insight into the way molecules rotate inside crystals. He and Ava Helen traveled to Europe again for several months, this time taking Linus, Jr., with them. His reputation growing, he was offered a prestigious faculty appointment at Harvard but turned it down. He did not feel at home on the East Coast, a place, he said, "where there were a lot of important people who were important just because of their birth. They had money and stature not based on their own abilities. I thought I would be a sort of second-class citizen at Harvard." Pauling was a westerner at heart, in love with a land where someone's worth was determined by what he did, not which family he was born into.

Again and again between 1928 and 1930 Pauling came back to the question of how to make the wave equation work for larger molecules. He was not alone. Heitler and London were trying to extend their work as well, although they were hindered by their limited knowledge of chemistry. A brilliant young physicist at MIT, John Slater, was also working on the problem, and in 1930 he found a clever, relatively simple way to use the wave equation to describe the *shape* of the patterns that electrons made in larger atoms like carbon. According to Slater's work on carbon, the areas certain electrons concentrated in—their orbitals—were not perfect spheres but stuck out from the atomic nucleus like stubby arms.

Slater's discovery spurred Pauling to make another push toward an answer in the fall of 1930. For weeks he sat at the desk of his small home study and wrote page after page of equations, trying to find an approximation, a shortcut to make the mathematics workable. His only result was frustration.

The breakthrough came late on a December night. He was working on a paradox in the carbon atom, trying to form a picture of it by adding up the wave equations for the separate electrons. Carbon has six electrons, two of which, according to the rules of quantum physics, would be paired in an orbital close to the nucleus, unavailable for any reaction. The other four would be split into different orbitals: two closer to the nucleus, the other two in orbitals that formed the stubby arms Slater had described. All four were available for forming bonds to other atoms. But because there were two types of orbitals involved, the bonds would be expected to be different as well. Chemists, however, knew that carbon most often formed four *identical* bonds to other atoms to form a perfect tetrahedron. How could the chemists' four identical bonds form when the physicists said that no four electrons in carbon were the same?

On that December evening, Pauling was trying to resolve the conundrum by using Heitler and London's electron exchange idea. He believed that the energy gained from the exchange when the carbon atom bound to others would be enough to break carbon's outer electrons out of their original energy levels and combine them into new forms, ones that would explain the tetrahedral binding of carbon. He called these new mixed forms hybrid orbitals.

That was fine in theory, but Pauling needed the mathematics to back him up. For months he worked on adding up Schrödinger's wave equation for the separate electrons of carbon to make his hybrids, but nothing seemed to give the right answer. He tried shortcuts, simplifications, and approximations—all leading to dead ends and wrong answers. But on this night he found the key. In yet another attempt to simplify the mathematics, he chose to leave out a part of the wave equation that he assumed was approximately the same for all the orbitals. If something is the same on both sides of an equation, he thought, you should be able to factor it out.

So Pauling dropped a section of the mathematics—and found the shortcut he needed. With that layer of complexity gone, the equations began to fall into place. He scribbled, erased, scribbled some more, and suddenly had an answer. He had created, from the principles and equations of quantum mechanics, a description of the tetrahedral binding of carbon. Everything he had calculated added up: the bond angles, lengths, strengths. He had pushed Heitler and London's concept to a new level.

But Pauling did not stop there. Using his simplified approach, he could add more electrons to his calculations and derive more complicated molecules. "I was so excited and happy, I think I stayed up all night, making, writing out, solving the equations, which were so simple I could solve them in a few minutes," he remembered. "Solve one equation, get the answer, then solve another equation. . . . I just kept getting more and more euphorious as time went by."

Two months later, Pauling sent his results to the *Journal of the American Chemical Society*. His paper, which he titled "The Nature of the Chemical Bond," showed chemists clearly, for the first time, how the new quantum mechanics could answer questions about the structure, magnetic properties, and bond strengths of molecules. Its publication in 1931 again brought Pauling international attention and showed the world that he was not only an extraordinary crystallographer but an accomplished chemical theorist. Later that year, he was awarded the American Chemical Society's Langmuir Prize as the best young chemist in the nation, a great honor capped by Arthur Amos Noyes's calling him "the most promising young man with whom I have ever come in contact in my many years of teaching." Caltech, realizing what a prize Pauling was, promoted him to full professor at age 30 and increased his salary.

The confidence others had in him was matched by Pauling's self-confidence. He now believed he could rebuild chemistry on a new foundation, using the wave equation

text continues on page 54

After finishing his first paper on the nature of the chemical bond, in 1931, Linus Pauling stopped basing his ideas on mathematical proofs. Chemists, he understood, were not trained to appreciate the difficult mathematics of quantum physics. To communicate with them, he developed his own theoretical style, made up in equal parts of a broad application of Erwin Schrödinger's wave mechanics, structural data from X-ray crystallography, other laboratory results from across the field of chemistry, and Pauling's own insights.

Observers termed Pauling's approach *semiempirical,* meaning that it was neither pure theory nor the simple marshaling of laboratory results. Whatever it was, it was tremendously successful. Using it, Pauling was able to answer long-standing questions about the nature of molecules, show that chemical bonds existed in a range of forms never imagined before, and rebuild chemistry on a new foundation provided by quantum mechanics.

Of all the world's scientists, only Pauling in the 1930s could fit together all these pieces of the puzzle. When he came up with a new idea about the chemical bond, he could immediately test it by comparing his thought structures with real ones discovered in his crystallography laboratory. And when a crystallographer proposed a new structure, Pauling could see if it was reasonable according to the rules of quantum mechanics. He constantly checked and cross-checked all of his new theoretical ideas against the known properties of molecules, their melting and boiling points, reactivity, and thermodynamic behavior.

Guiding Pauling's work was his fervent belief that molecular function was explained by molecular structure. Molecules had their own architecture, measured in billionths of inches, and Pauling's great drive was to be the first to describe as many of these structures as possible—thereby gaining new understanding about how they behaved.

text continued from page 52

and his belief in molecular structure to test old theories, devise new experiments, and come up with new insights. During the next five years he did just that, presenting his results in a series of groundbreaking papers on the nature of the chemical bond.

But his following papers were different. In them, Pauling turned away from rigorous mathematical proofs of his ideas, relying instead on his intuitive understanding of physics and chemistry to guide him. He developed his own style, using the best of wave mechanics theory with hard data about molecular structure from X-ray crystallography.

Of all the world's scientists, only Pauling could at that time in the 1930s take these two pieces of the puzzle and use one to clarify the other. When he came up with a new theory about the chemical bond, he could immediately test it by comparing his thought-structures with real ones

Pauling lecturing at Caltech in 1935. His energetic, funny, and informal way of teaching won the hearts of generations of students.

discovered in his crystallography laboratory. When a crystallographer came up with a puzzling bit of hard data, Pauling could decide whether to heed it or not by passing it through the test of quantum mechanics. No one else could blend physics and chemistry, theory and laboratory results like Pauling could, dancing gracefully between one and the other. No one else embodied the proper balance of memory, understanding, imagination, and hard work.

Pauling's approach worked especially well for mathematics-shy chemists. He wrote his papers without complicated equations, depending instead on applying what he knew to the questions that chemists most wanted answered. He presented his ideas in ways that fit with a chemist's understanding of nature, using real-world examples and freely borrowing what he was learning about the structure of molecules to check his theories and make his points.

Historians would later credit Heitler, London, Slater, and Pauling with developing this approach to the chemical bond (in later years it would be called, in their honor, the HLSP theory). But most chemists would remember only Pauling, not only because he applied it to more molecules than the others, but because he alone among them was a chemist, able to communicate his results in a way that chemists understood.

By 1936, Pauling had used his approach to explain everything from the structure of benzene to the properties of metals, and he felt that he understood almost everything he needed to know about the chemical bond. His self-confidence, which had been growing since he went to Oregon Agricultural College, now assumed legendary proportions. He was the brightest young star in the world of chemistry, and he behaved like it. He had a new private office, a larger laboratory, and twice the number of graduate students and postdoctoral fellows of any other Caltech chemist. He traveled often, teaching one term each year at Berkeley (where he became friends with G. N. Lewis, whose papers had first interested him in the chemical bond) and giving lectures around the nation on what was now being called "quantum chemistry."

Pauling had always been a very good teacher, but now he had a bravado all his own. He was "a bouncy young extrovert," as one student saw him during a visit to the University of Chicago in the mid-1930s, "wholly informal in dress and appearance. He bounded into the room, already crowded with students eager to see and hear the Great Man, spread himself over the seminar table next to the blackboard and, running his hand through an unruly shock of hair, gestured to the students to come closer. . . . The talk started with Pauling leaping off the table and rapidly writing a list of five topics on which he could speak singly or all together. He described each in a few pithy sentences, including racy impressions of the workers involved."

Through it all, he retained a wonderful appreciation for the equality of all people. He was as informal, charming, and funny with student dishwashers in a laboratory as he was with august professors heading the university. He discriminated not on the basis of title, but of intelligence: His only requirements for instant friendship seemed to be that the person be as wide awake, open-minded, and (almost) as quick-witted as he was.

Still, not everyone was charmed. Pauling's rapid rise rankled some older members of the Caltech chemistry division. To them, the young man—whom they still remembered as a penniless graduate student—appeared to have become something of a prima donna. Pauling's enormous self-assurance, his new love of parties and travel, and his habit of lampooning less brilliant scientists were part of the problem. To some, Pauling's ebullient, irreverent manner was undignified. There was more than a bit of jealousy involved, but more important were the concerns that Pauling was not a team player. During the financial crisis of the Great Depression, when money was hard to find at

Caltech, Pauling seemed interested in pushing for funds only for his own rapidly expanding laboratory, without thinking about the needs of the whole division.

The anti-Pauling concerns came to a head when Noyes developed cancer in the spring of 1936, bringing up the question of a successor. "King Arthur" believed that when choosing a leader for a research group his scientific potential was more important than his seniority. Of all his faculty, he believed that only Pauling had the creative spark to open new fields of research, the talent to attract much-needed new funds, and the energy to continue pushing Caltech's chemistry department to the forefront of American science. Noyes was not blind to Pauling's faults—he called him "restless, ambitious and self-seeking" in a letter to a friend—but the balance sheet favored Pauling. Noyes wanted the young star to succeed him as head of the Caltech chemistry division.

After Noyes's death, however, Pauling's ascent to the chairmanship of the division was not a foregone conclusion. The older faculty immediately brought Pauling's "dictatorial tendencies" to the attention of Caltech's head, Robert Millikan—who thought Pauling too young for a chairmanship in any case—and made certain that Pauling was the only member of the chemistry division not asked to be an honorary pallbearer at Noyes's funeral. Pauling's appointment as chemistry division chair was delayed for months, a development that hurt and confused Pauling. He had put all of his time into doing some of the best chemistry research in the world. It was true that he had not cultivated friendships with many of the other professors. But how could his success lead to such a reaction? He held proudly aloof during this period, waiting for Millikan to come to him with an offer. But despite Noyes's wishes, Millikan refused to make Pauling chair of the division.

It took the intervention of one of the most powerful men in science to break the impasse. Warren Weaver was the head of the natural sciences division of the world's wealthiest philanthropy, the Rockefeller Foundation, a position that made him what one historian called "the chief banker for American science." Rockefeller money built universities and careers and, especially during the Great Depression, was critical to keeping many science programs afloat, including those at Caltech.

Weaver had a particular interest in Pauling, because he recognized that the young chemist's abilities might help him reach a treasured goal: to successfully apply the techniques of chemistry and physics to the field of biology. Weaver believed that biology was out of date. He thought it needed intellectual rigor and new experimental techniques focused on the molecular workings of the body. If the molecules and reactions that led to life could be described and controlled, he believed, it might be possible to create a superior race of humans that were more rational, more intelligent. He even coined a phrase to describe the field he intended to fund: molecular biology.

Pauling's brilliant work had caught Weaver's eye in the early 1930s, and by the time Noyes died, he had already used great amounts of research money to turn the young man's interests from the structure of minerals to important biological molecules such as proteins. Weaver also felt that Pauling should be in charge of the Caltech chemistry program. So, after months dragged by, Weaver decided to take matters into his own hands. He took a train to Pasadena, talked with both Pauling and Millikan, and convinced them both, for the good of the Institute, to give a little ground and start talking to each other. A short time after returning to New York, Weaver received a letter from Pauling. "After talking with you I went to Professor Millikan determined to straighten out our misunderstandings. We reached an agreement with very little difficulty and I am sure that everyone is pleased."

In 1937, at the age of 36, Linus Pauling was named chairman of one of the most important chemistry programs in the world. As it turned out, the worries of the older faculty members proved overblown. Under Pauling's leadership, a great era in chemistry began at Caltech. Holmes Sturdivant, his former graduate student, became his right-hand man, efficiently handling most routine matters. Pauling directed the big picture, traveling, lecturing, raising money, and overseeing the general direction of research. All the major decisions within the chemistry division were made by majority vote, ensuring that Pauling's alleged "dictatorial" tendencies never became a problem. His friendship with Weaver kept Rockefeller money flowing in. Students flocked to Pasadena, eager to work with the man whose achievements had made him one of the world's most famous chemists. Despite the grumbling of some faculty members, Pauling's ability to attract money and his hands-off style of administration kept the division running smoothly and growing quickly. And with all that, he continued to make brilliant discoveries, either on his own or in conjunction with one of his many graduate students or postdoctoral fellows.

In the fall of 1937, the new chairman and Ava Helen left Pasadena to spend four months at Cornell University in

In 1937, Pauling (front row, center) was named chairman of Caltech's chemistry department. Some of the older faculty members thought that Pauling was too young for such a position.

THE SIGNIFICANCE OF STRUCTURAL CHEMISTRY

by Linus Pauling.

Introductory lecture of the George Fisher Baker Lectureship in Chemistry, Cornell University. 8:15 P.M., Tuesday, October 12, 1937. Also used at Pomona, 8 P.M. March 10, 1938, under the title "THE STRUCTURAL CHEMISTRY OF BLOOD".

President Day, ladies and gentlemen: Before beginning the discussion of the topic for the evening, "The Significance of Structural Chemistry", I wish to thank the University and especially the members of the Department of Chemistry for their kindness in extending to me an invitation to present the George Fisher Baker Lectures for the present academic year. It is indeed a great honor and privilege to speak and work in this wonderful laboratory, as well as a great pleasure to spend some months on this beautiful campus.

I have seen on looking over the books published by earlier Baker Lecturers that in most cases the Lecturer has chosen for the topic of his Introductory Address some philosophical, economic, or political question. After much thought I have abandoned the idea of doing this, in part because I have been unable to think of any such topic to which I feel I could make a significant contribution. Remembering, however, the statement of Aristotle, " Old men should be politicians, young men mathematicians"; I have decided to speak about the subject of structural chemistry, to which I have devoted most of my professional attention for fifteen years.

In his "Mathematical Theory of Relativity," Eddington wrote "The investigation of the external world in physics is a quest for structure rather than substance." This is true in the main not only for physicists but for all scientific

Pauling's handwritten notes for a series of lectures he delivered at Cornell University in 1937. These lectures were published in 1939 as The Nature of the Chemical Bond, a book that is now considered one of the century's most important scientific works.

Ithaca, New York, where he had been asked to deliver the George Fisher Baker lectures. This prestigious appointment involved giving a series of talks on a single subject, which would then be published as a volume in the Baker series. Pauling's lectures on the chemical bond were a great success. After returning to Caltech in early 1938, he spent the next few months reworking and expanding his notes.

The result was published in 1939 as *The Nature of the Chemical Bond and the Structure of Molecules and Crystals: An Introduction to Modern Structural Chemistry*. It would become the most important Baker lecture book ever printed, and one of the most-cited scientific texts in history. In a very basic way, this book changed the course of chemistry. For the first time, the discipline was explained not as a collection of facts tied together by practical application in the laboratory but as a field unified by an underlying physical theory: Pauling's quantum-mechanical ideas about the chemical bond. By showing how the new physics explained the chemical bond, how those bonds explained the structure of molecules, and how molecules' structure explained their behavior, Pauling showed for the first time, as the Nobel Prize–winner Max Perutz said, that "chemistry could be understood rather than memorized."

The response from readers was immediate and enthusiastic. G. N. Lewis's comments were typical, if somewhat more lighthearted than most. He wrote Pauling, "I have just returned from a short vacation for which the only books I took were half a dozen detective stories and your 'Chemical Bond.' I found yours the most exciting of the lot." Chemistry professors began assigning the book to their graduate students. Sales went well, continuing to grow for decades as the book went through many printings and three editions. Over the next 20 years, *The Nature of the Chemical Bond* would become established as a classic.

Pauling with his wife, Ava Helen, and four children on the steps of their Pasadena home shortly before the start of World War II. The demands of Pauling's work kept him from being a close and nurturing father.

A Scientist at War

Linus Pauling's success as chairman of the Caltech Division of Chemistry and Chemical Engineering was due in no small part to a steady flow of funding from the Rockefeller Foundation. Warren Weaver, the foundation's director of funding for natural sciences, had focused Pauling's attention on the new field of molecular biology and had given him large sums of research money through the late 1930s. The funding was provided to study the structure of biomolecules, the enzymes and genes, antibodies and hormones that had such profound and mysterious effects in the body. Weaver capped his support in 1936 with a magnificent gift: a quarter of a million dollars to staff and equip a new Caltech building devoted to bio-organic chemistry. The new facility's spacious laboratories, equipped with the latest and most expensive equipment, and the outstanding scientists who came to work there would be under Pauling's command.

This new building was named the Crellin Laboratory, after Edward Crellin, a retired steel magnate who had given millions to Caltech. Pauling was so pleased with it that he and Ava Helen named their fourth child, born just as the building was nearing completion, Edward Crellin Pauling.

"Crellie," as he would be called, would be the last of Linus and Ava Helen's children, joining older brothers Linus, Jr., and Peter and sister Linda. To accommodate the growing tribe, Pauling built a large, rambling, ranch-style home on a hillside overlooking a beautiful arroyo outside Pasadena. It was a house that reflected the man, designed for comfort, not show. There were two large wings, one for the children and another for the adults, joined in the middle at exactly the angle formed by carbon atoms in benzene, and fronted with adobe brick. There were bookcases everywhere, a big fireplace in the living room, an octagonal study for Pauling, a garden space for Ava Helen, and plenty of room for the children to play.

As the 1930s ended, the Paulings' lives took on a routine. Pauling had breakfast with the family and left for the laboratory, sometimes driving the kids to school on the way. Ava Helen tended house. After a morning's work overseeing his laboratory, doing minor administrative work, and attending meetings, Pauling would eat lunch at home or at the Athenaeum, Caltech's elegant faculty club. In the afternoon, he would return to his office, handle major divisional matters, and write grant requests and papers. He always spent suppertime with the family. When it was over, Pauling would disappear into his study, where he would listen to the news on the radio, read scientific journals, popular magazines, and newspapers, write a bit, and dictate letters and memoranda until going to bed at about 11:00.

On the weekends, Pauling spent almost all his time in the study. He would emerge only when he heard Ava Helen ringing the doorbell to call him to meals. The children, under strict orders not to make noise or bother their father, saw little of him. Crellin remembered when he was little, listening through the study door as Pauling dictated letters on the other side and wondering who the person was named "Comma" that his father always talked to.

Pauling worked terrifically hard, twelve hours a day, seven days a week, including most holidays, but it did not seem like hard work to him. He was doing what he loved and, like any artist, he found that the hours he spent thinking about new discoveries passed quickly. He loved reading and was proud of his ability to keep abreast of the latest developments in many fields, not only chemistry and physics but now, as his interests turned to molecular biology, in biochemistry, the study of enzymes and viruses, and research into blood molecules. All this he stored away in his capacious memory, ready to be called upon when needed to make new connections.

When Pauling had new ideas—and sometimes he had two or three per day—he usually jotted them down in a short memo and passed them on to a growing group of research assistants, postdoctoral fellows, and graduate students for verification in the laboratory. When, as was usually the case, his ideas were found to be right, a paper would appear in the scientific press, in which Pauling shared credit with his many coworkers.

The results seemed almost magical. No one had Pauling's wide range of knowledge and his nearly intuitive understanding of how atoms liked to join together. No one had yet mastered his technique of model building guided by strict chemical rules. With these tools, Pauling was able to produce an enormous body of work in the late 1930s, on everything from the structure of ice to the magnetic properties of hemoglobin, from the significance of resonance in molecules to the nature of metals, from the uses of electron diffraction to a theory of the color of dyes.

But of all Pauling's work during this period, nothing was more important than his attempt to understand the structure of some of the most complex and important molecules on earth: the proteins. Hair and feathers, skin and muscle are proteins, as are the major parts of nerves and the chromosomes that carry the secret of heredity. Enzymes, biomolecules that have a strange ability to speed certain reactions, are proteins; antibodies that fight off infections are proteins; the hemoglobin that carries oxygen in the blood is a protein. Proteins are involved in every major reaction and form an important part of every major structure of the body.

It was here, at the level of proteins, Pauling and many others believed, that dead chemicals somehow were transformed into moving, breathing organisms. Whoever discovered how proteins were built and worked, the thinking went, would discover the secret of life. Pauling intended to do just that.

But proteins were a nightmare to study. Proteins appeared to vary widely in size, and some were gigantic, consisting of tens of thousands of atoms joined into molecules that were orders of magnitude larger than anything Pauling had studied before. They were so huge that Pauling estimated that solving even the simplest would take 50 years using X-ray crystallography alone. They were also difficult to purify and easy to mangle. Even modest heating, mild treatment with acids or alkalis, or just mechanical agitation like beating eggwhites with a fork could be enough to change a protein's properties and kill its activity. This process was called denaturation.

Denaturation made proteins difficult to study, but it also offered a doorway to understanding them. Pauling was interested to read the work of two Rockefeller Institute scientists who had found that some proteins could be denatured by gentle heating, but then could, if cooled properly, regain their original activity. Higher heat, however, irreversibly denatured the molecules, seemingly broke them into pieces so that nothing would return them to an active state.

This characteristic meant that denaturation was a two-step process. It also gave Pauling an idea. The two steps in denaturation—the first, reversible step caused by gentle

Pauling in his Caltech laboratory in 1940. Despite the many demands made on his time as the head of the chemistry department, Pauling continued to conduct groundbreaking research on his own.

heat and the second, irreversible one caused by higher heat—could mean the involvement of two kinds of chemical bonds: the first, relatively weak bonds easily broken and re-formed and the second, stronger bonds, harder to break and impossible to remake.

Pauling had a guess about the weaker bonds. In his reading he had come across a description of a so-called hydrogen bond, a very weak link in which a hydrogen atom acted as a bridge between two others. The original work with the hydrogen bond had been done with water molecules, and no one thought it was important in any other setting. But Pauling saw that the estimated strength of the hydrogen bond fit the data about the first level of denaturation. He then began thinking about how hydrogen bonds might work in proteins.

It was already known from the work of the German organic chemist Emil Fischer that proteins also contained strong covalent bonds formed by the equal sharing of pairs of electrons between two atoms. If these stronger bonds were broken, the protein would fall into pieces. Covalent bonds would take more energy to break, and when broken, could not easily be re-formed. This might represent the second level of denaturation.

To test his ideas, Pauling lured Alfred Mirsky, one of the Rockefeller scientists studying proteins, to Pasadena and started him working on a series of studies designed to measure carefully the energy needed at each step of denaturation. Mirsky liked Pauling's ideas, which meshed nicely with Fischer's theory that proteins were made of long chains of amino acids linked end to end. Each time one amino acid linked to another, a water molecule was given off and a specific kind of covalent bond, which Fischer called a peptide bond, was formed. Long strings of amino acids could be formed, which Fischer called polypeptide ("many peptide") chains. These chains could be looped or twisted around, Pauling thought, and pinned into specific shapes through the formation of weaker hydrogen bonds between different parts of the chain.

Pauling and Mirsky published their ideas in a 1936 paper that became a milestone in the history of protein science. "Our conception of a native protein molecule (showing specific properties) is the following," they wrote. "The molecule consists of one polypeptide chain which continues without interruption throughout the molecule. . . . This chain is folded into a uniquely defined configuration, in which it is held by hydrogen bonds." This, they wrote, was the basic structure of all proteins.

Their idea explained the two levels of denaturation. The first step consisted of breaking hydrogen bonds, which would unfold the protein strings, leading to a loss of native activity. As long as the strings were in one piece, however, the hydrogen bonds could re-form, returning the molecule to its original shape and activity. Treat it more harshly, however, and the covalent peptide bonds along the string would break, leading to irreversible denaturation.

This analysis cleverly explained denaturation, but it did more. Pauling and Mirsky were proposing that all proteins were basically the same at one level—they were all long chains of amino acids—but differed in their abilities because of their final shape. It was the shape of the protein that determined its specific properties, they argued: Molecular shape was the secret of life.

But what were those shapes, and how did they confer on proteins their amazing abilities? How did an enzyme's molecular form explain its ability to catalyze one, and only one, specific chemical reaction? How did a gene's shape explain its ability to make exact copies of itself?

These were big questions, and Pauling began searching for answers in a variety of ways. He thought first of building a model of proteins, working upward from what little was known of the structure of amino acids, the basic units of protein chains. He set a hard-working, meticulous assistant, Robert Corey, to work using X-ray crystallography to discover the structure of the simplest amino acid, glycine. When Corey quickly succeeded—becoming the first person ever to describe with precision how an amino acid is built—Pauling put him to work on a two-amino-acid molecule called diketopiperizine. The goal here was to determine for the first time the precise length and angle of the peptide bond. Pauling had a hunch that this particular bond would prove critical to understanding protein structures, because he theorized from what he knew about amino acids that it held the atoms on either side of it in a very specific, quite rigid way. If that was true, it would reduce greatly the possible number of ways in which protein chains could fold and twist. Corey's work confirmed Pauling's prediction.

While the two learned more about these building blocks, Pauling was also working to understand more about the properties of whole proteins. In the spring of 1936 Pauling had met Karl Landsteiner, a distinguished, silver-haired, Austrian-born researcher who had won a Nobel Prize for discovering how to make transfusions safe by testing for blood types. Landsteiner's passion was immunology, the study of the body's defense mechanisms against infection and disease, with a special focus on antibodies, which were

text continues on page 72

Pauling's protein model was not the only one generating interest during the 1930s. The same year that he and protein researcher Alfred Mirsky published their ideas on denaturation, a brilliant and unconventional British scientist gained worldwide attention with her own, very different, ideas about proteins.

Dorothy Wrinch, the first woman to receive a doctorate in science from Oxford, was in many ways ahead of her time. She spoke her mind (often with an acid tongue), smoked cigarettes, believed in independent careers for married women, and forcefully pursued her own. Trained as a mathematician, Wrinch believed that all scientific progress grew directly out of pure logic; she found her greatest success applying that approach to biology.

In the early 1930s, Wrinch was an intellectual gypsy, separated from her physicist husband, traveling through Europe with her young daughter, apprenticing at biological laboratories to learn about embryology, genetics, and protein structure. Her mathematical approach attracted the attention of the Rockefeller Foundation's Warren Weaver, who in 1935 gave her a grant to fund her work for five years.

She used the time to devise an intriguing set of ideas about protein structures. Starting with the then-popular (but mistaken) idea that many proteins were composed of subunits numbering exactly 288 amino acids, Wrinch constructed models that were not long chains, like Pauling's, but fabrics formed by amino acids connected in more complex ways. Her favorite was a honeycomb of hexagonal rings that could be folded around on itself to make a cagelike structure of exactly 288 amino acids. She called it a cyclol.

Wrinch's cyclol was appealing because it had a three-dimensional shape with an outside and an inside, a general configuration that many protein researchers believed was likely for a lot of important proteins. But Pauling was skeptical. He did not believe that nature dictated any "magic numbers" such as 288 amino acids for proteins, and did not think that the types of chemical bonds that Wrinch proposed for cyclols were likely to exist. After talking with Wrinch and discovering how little she knew about protein

Dorothy Wrinch (right) shows a model of her cyclol structure to two colleagues. Pauling was skeptical of her work and published a paper demolishing Wrinch's arguments.

chemistry, he wrote Weaver a stinging report that concluded that Wrinch's "arguments are sometimes unreliable and her information superficial."

Still, because so little good evidence was available about protein structure in general, there was no direct proof that Wrinch was wrong. Free to theorize, she continued to make her case through the late 1930s, earning the support of some well-known scientists and even appearing in front-page news items in which reporters called her the woman Einstein.

To put an end to what he saw as a distraction from more valuable lines of inquiry, Pauling and fellow protein researcher Carl Niemann in 1939 published a paper marshaling all the chemical evidence in favor of their chain theory of protein structure and against Wrinch's arguments. Its impact was devastating. After it appeared, no one would take Wrinch's cyclols seriously again.

Pauling and Niemann turned out to be right—mostly. Pauling's chains would prove the rule in nature, cyclols the extremely rare exception. Pauling would go on to win world acclaim, Wrinch to spend the rest of her life in scientific obscurity, arguing for her structures, reminding anyone who would listen how Pauling had undermined her work and calling him "a most dangerous fellow."

text continued from page 69

blood proteins that had the unique ability to recognize and latch onto specific targets like viruses and bacteria, clump them into masses, and help clear them from the body.

Antibodies, Landsteiner told Pauling, posed an intriguing puzzle. They were all proteins, all roughly the same size and shape, and all made of roughly the same mix of amino acids, yet each was also very different in the way it attached to one and only one target molecule, or antigen. An antibody to a certain virus would not attach strongly to anything else. Landsteiner had found that a single animal could form thousands of different antibodies, including new ones for synthetic chemicals never found in nature.

Knowing of Pauling's work on denaturation, Landsteiner asked for his help. Could Pauling, with his knowledge of structural chemistry, explain how similar proteins could recognize and bind to so many different antigens in this bafflingly precise way?

Pauling had no quick answer. He bought a copy of Landsteiner's book on antibodies, quickly read it, and spent time thinking. His first assumption was, of course, that molecular structure had to be involved. The shapes of antibodies would determine their specificity. But how?

In 1940, Pauling published a brilliant answer. Each antibody molecule, he theorized, was formed by the body as a denatured chain, stretched out, without hydrogen bonds, with no specific shape. One end would then come into contact with a foreign molecule, an antigen, and begin to shape itself around it. It would be held in place by weak bonds: hydrogen bonds, the attraction of oppositely charged areas on the surface of the antigen and antibody, and so forth. Like soft clay being pressed onto a coin, the antibody would take on a complementary shape, and when that shape was good enough, the fit close enough, the sum of all the weak links would be great enough so that antibody and antigen would stick together. The same thing could happen at the other end of the antibody chain, making a "bivalent" molecule capable of latching onto two foreign molecules at once, explaining how antibodies could clump their targets together.

It was a wonderful theory, but it was in part very wrong. The idea that antibodies are created as denatured proteins that become specific by adapting their shape through direct contact to antigens would prove to be mistaken. But the underlying concept of key-in-lock complementary shapes causing an antibody to stick to a target was right.

For 15 years, however, until a new, more powerful theory of antibody formation was put forward, Pauling's idea led the field. His antibody work again expanded his growing reputation as a master of many fields.

But at the height of his success, his world began to fall apart.

In the late 1930s Pauling, like many other American scientists, began to receive increasingly desperate letters from colleagues in Germany. The researchers, many of them Jewish, were seeking someone, anyone, who could help them escape the Nazis by obtaining a visa for travel to America. Pauling, who personally knew many German researchers through his European travels, became keenly aware of the anti-Jewish, antiscience attitudes of Hitler and his government. By 1939, Pauling was convinced that Hitler had to be stopped.

With Ava Helen's encouragement, he began speaking out about the issue and joined a group called Union Now that proposed joining all the democracies in the world into a federation modeled on that of the United States. At first Pauling was a bit uncomfortable speaking on political topics, but he soon found he enjoyed it. When Germany attacked France and then Britain, he began speaking passionately in junior high school auditoriums and local living rooms about the need for America to help. "Should not our country help Britain now to fight off the thing which is attacking her and will probably attack us when she is polished off?" he asked his audiences. "This means going to

PASADENA
EXECUTIVE COMMITTEE

Lee Shippey
 Chairman

Clark B. Millikan
 Secretary

M. W. deLaubenfels
 Speakers' Bureau

W. Jarvis Barlow
Theodore Dunham, Jr.
Bessie Little
Elizabeth Page
Linus Pauling
Robert A. Waring

NATIONAL
EXECUTIVE COMMITTEE

Clarence K. Streit
 Chairman

Frank Aydelotte
William P. Blake
 Corresponding Secretary

Lowell H. Brown
Russell Davenport
Henry S. Dennison
James E. Downes
Gordon Mannerstedt
Vernon Nash
R. Frazier Potts
 Manager

Ernest H. Wilkins

INTER-DEMOCRACY
FEDERAL UNIONISTS

For UNION NOW of Democratic Nations . . . as the Nucleus of a
World Government . . . of, by, and for the People

"Now it is proposed to form a Government for men and not for Societies of men or States."
GEORGE MASON in the Constitutional Convention of the American Union, 1787

PASADENA COMMITTEE
40 SOUTH OAK KNOLL AVENUE, PASADENA, CALIFORNIA
TELEPHONE: SYCAMORE 2-4831

February 1, 1940

To all interested in "Union Now":

    The Pasadena Local Committee of Inter-Democracy Federal Unionists
was formally organized at an open meeting at the Public Library on
December 12, 1939. A telegram from National Headquarters was read at
this meeting, stating that the Charter for the Pasadena Committee had
been approved and formally ratified. Dr. Soares (the temporary Chairman)
appointed a committee to elect officers to serve for a preliminary period.
This committee met and elected officers as follows: Chairman, Lee Shippey;
Vice-Chairman, Theodore Dunham, Jr.; Secretary, Clark Millikan; Treasurer,
Robert Waring. There have been three public meetings for "Union Now" under
the auspices of the local committee, with an average attendance of over 200.

    Talks on the plan for a Federal Union of the Democracies have been
given in Pasadena and surrounding communities, before a variety of organizations, by a number of our members, in particular Miss Elizabeth Page,
M. W. deLaubenfels, Lee Shippey, Graham Laing, Linus Pauling, Robert Waring,
and Mrs. Clark Millikan. In every instance the response of audiences has
been most enthusiastic.

    Through the great generosity of a member, space has been made
available for a Headquarters at 40 South Oak Knoll Avenue, Pasadena.
There will be a telephone (SYcamore 2-4831) and a supply of literature
at this office, which will be open daily from 10 to 12, and from 3 to 5.
If some of our members can lend a long table, a desk, a chair or two, and
a book-case, to furnish this Headquarters, it will be greatly appreciated.
A typewriter would also be useful.

    There is to be a special meeting at the house of Miss Dorothy
Carlson, 1783 North El Molino Avenue, on Thursday, February 8th, at 8 P.M.,
for those who wish to take an active part in the work of the Committee.
Please come if you would like to help. There are jobs for all.

    Don't forget the meeting on Monday evening.

Lee Shippey
Theodore Dunham, Jr.
Linus Pauling

"For the great Republic, for the principle it lives by and keeps alive, for man's vast future." —ABRAHAM LINCOLN

*Pauling served on the executive committee of Pasadena's chapter of Union Now, a group that proposed
joining all the world's democracies into a world government to fight Hitler.*

war, and we, as idealists, are by nature pacifists and opposed to war. But we are being forced into war anyway. . . . It is the cancerous growth of Nazism—of dictatorship in general—that must be eradicated from the otherwise orderly organism of the world."

Pauling's anti-Nazi sentiments were shared by many high-ranking officials. Even before declaring war, the U.S. government began preparing by mobilizing scientists to help solve a number of technical problems plaguing the military. Pauling was eager to do anything he could. In October 1940, he joined 30 other chemists in a Washington, D.C., meeting with army and navy officers and heard a wish list of military needs, including requests for new medicines and better explosives. The navy had a particular problem: Their submarine force was plagued by an inability to measure oxygen levels accurately, a deficiency that led to either too much oxygen, risking an explosion, or too little, leading to drowsy submariners.

On the way back to Pasadena on the train, Pauling brainstormed a way to make an accurate oxygen meter. The trick was to take advantage of the fact that oxygen, alone of all the common gases, was attracted to a magnet. When he got home, Pauling had an assistant put together a device that suspended within a sample of the air to be tested a tiny, delicately balanced hollow tube filled with a normal concentration of oxygen. The entire setup was then put between the ends of a horseshoe magnet. Any change in the magnetic behavior of the air sample being tested would affect how the hollow tube turned in the magnetic field, a change that could be read out on a dial. The system he devised worked, and the Pauling Oxygen Analyzer was soon in production at Caltech.

Then Pauling's war efforts were sidelined by illness. On a trip to New York in March 1941 to receive an award, he noticed that his energy was flagging and his joints seemed to be swelling. His shoes and shirt collars were tight, his eyes swollen shut in the morning. Alarmed, he saw a doctor.

The diagnosis was Bright's disease, a serious progressive ailment that prevents the kidneys from properly filtering the blood. The outlook was not good, his doctors told him. Bright's disease almost always damaged the kidneys so severely that the patient died. Shaken, Pauling and Ava Helen returned to Pasadena, where Pauling decided that he was going to fight for his life. He put himself under the care of a brilliant, individualistic kidney specialist he had heard about named Thomas Addis. Addis had his own theory about Bright's disease, and had developed a dietary method of treatment that most of his medical colleagues thought nonsense. But Pauling had nothing to lose. Soon he was religiously following Addis's salt-free, protein-free dietary regimen, heavy with bananas and gelatin, supplemented with vitamins and minerals. Ava Helen made certain he never deviated, becoming her husband's nurse and dietitian, carefully weighing each portion of food, gauging the nutrient values, noting everything in a spiral notebook.

Amazingly, Addis's program seemed to work. After some weeks in bed, Pauling began working half-days. After four months his swelling was gone; after six months his mental and physical energy was returning to normal. "For many years after that," one of Pauling's friends recalled, "it seemed to me that he was getting younger every year instead of older." Pauling stayed on a low-protein diet for 15 years, attributing his survival and good health to Addis.

All his renewed energy went into the war effort. After the United States declared war in December 1941, Caltech's researchers turned from the structure of the universe to the design of munitions and defense materials. Pauling's laboratories became hives of research

In 1940, Pauling developed this oxygen meter that would allow submarines to accurately measure oxygen levels.

into explosives, rocket propellants, and artificial blood plasma for wounded soldiers. He traveled often, visiting munitions plants and providing scientific advice to government agencies. He codesigned and patented an armor-piercing shell. He even had a chance to join the most important project of the war, when J. Robert Oppenheimer invited Pauling to join the top-secret group at Los Alamos, New Mexico, that was working to develop the atomic bomb. Pauling, loath either to leave his family or relocate, declined the offer, "Not because I felt that it was wrong to work on the development of nuclear weapons," Pauling said, "rather that I had other jobs that I was doing."

The war years were not easy ones for the Pauling family. From the yard of their home in the hills above Pasadena, they could hear the booming explosions from Caltech's powder research labs. There were air-raid scares and food and fuel rationing. Ava Helen grew vegetables for the family in a home "Victory Garden," helped in a Caltech laboratory that was developing artificial rubber, and trained as an air-raid warden.

Pauling's wife also took a strong stand against the forced internment of West Coast Japanese Americans, who, in a government effort to prevent espionage and unrest during the war, were herded into what Ava Helen and others felt were American concentration camps. To protest this injustice, she began volunteering in the Los Angeles office of the American Civil Liberties Union, which was fighting the internment.

All this meant that the Pauling children saw less and less of their parents. Linus, Jr., after a troubled time settling down in high school, enlisted in the air corps and left home toward the end of the war. The other children felt varying degrees of loneliness and isolation.

The war was not easy on anyone. But sacrifices had to be made if Pauling's "orderly organism of the world" was to be made whole again.

The Triple Helix

On the morning of Tuesday, August 7, 1945, Linus Pauling stopped at a Pasadena drugstore to buy a newspaper. He would remember the next few moments for the rest of his life. The newspaper headline read, "Tokyo Admits Atomic Havoc." A new type of American bomb had just been dropped on the Japanese city of Hiroshima. An enormous fireball had killed or injured tens of thousands of Japanese. Much of the city, the report said, was destroyed in an instant. J. Robert Oppenheimer's experiment, the Los Alamos project he had tried to talk Pauling into joining, had been a success. Science had created the atomic bomb.

Three days later, Pauling read that another of the new weapons had destroyed the city of Nagasaki. Shortly after that, Japan surrendered. World War II was over. Americans danced in the streets, and Pauling and his family joined in the general euphoria.

But when the excitement wore off, Pauling and many other scientists were left with difficult questions. They began gathering in small groups, in private homes and faculty clubs, to talk about the social and political implications of the new bomb. A few dozen of these devices, delivered

A mushroom cloud rises over Nagasaki after an atomic bomb was detonated there on August 8, 1945. The power and destruction caused by this new weapon spurred Pauling and other scientists into political action to limit its development and use.

by airplanes, could destroy an entire nation, wiping out its armies and cities in a single day. Didn't the power of these weapons now make war obsolete? It made sense to have military secrets in wartime, but now there was peace. Should the workings of the atomic bomb remain military secrets, or should they now be shared, like any other scientific discoveries, with the rest of the world? Atomic energy could also be used to make electricity. Didn't scientists owe it to the war-ravaged planet to make that process available to everyone?

As more details about incinerated cities, terrible burns, and radiation poisoning became public, a sense of guilt was added to the scientists' other concerns. Wasn't it immoral to develop this weapon? What had they done?

Pauling joined a discussion group of concerned professors and students in Pasadena and was among the first to understand that the new bomb also meant a changed role for scientists. "The problem presented to the world by the destructive power of atomic energy overshadows, of course, any other problem," he wrote a fellow researcher less than two months after Hiroshima. "I feel that, in addition to our professional activities in the nuclear field, we should make our voices known with respect to the political significance of science."

This approach was something new, because scientists usually steered clear of politics. They were trained to be objective, to analyze data critically and fairly, and to come to conclusions uncolored by personal prejudice. But politics was messy, personal, and often rooted in emotions and partisanship. How could scientists be objective if they were taking political stands?

Pauling's answer, and that of hundreds of other scientists in the months just after the war, was that they must add their voices to the public debate over the bomb. Their objectivity and technological know-how was required to inform the political debate. The new bombs were complicated scientific discoveries that also had enormous political effects. The public needed to understand both how they worked and what they were capable of—as well as the positive side of the possible development of atomic power— if there was to be a rational use of this powerful new technology. Scientists were needed to explain all of this.

The Pasadena discussion group talked for hours over beer and pretzels in the basement of the Caltech faculty club about all these issues, including the inescapable reality that the United States would not long have a monopoly on the atomic bomb. As Albert Einstein said, "What nature tells one group of men, she will tell in time to any group interested and patient enough in asking the questions." If the Soviet Union and other nations developed the bomb, as Pauling was certain they soon would, what was to prevent a worldwide holocaust?

The answer, hundreds of scientists nationwide agreed, was logical. No one nation could keep atomic secrets, so they should be shared with all. As Einstein began pointing out, the new bombs were a signal that humankind needed a new form of government, a cooperative world body that would not only oversee the peaceful development of atomic power but quash any individual nation foolish enough to threaten atomic war.

Pauling and many other scientists began to speak out on these issues. Dozens of scientists' discussion groups coalesced into a national organization, the Federation of Atomic Scientists (FAS), which lobbied Congress to keep atomic energy under civilian rather than military control. Pauling joined the FAS and raised his voice in favor of civilian control.

To help further involve the public in atomic energy issues, Einstein and a small group of other leading researchers formed the Emergency Committee of Atomic Scientists to raise money for public information campaigns. Pauling was happy to join when asked, especially because

Pauling in 1949 at Caltech's faculty club, the Athenaeum. Pauling's increasing involvement in antiwar activities would isolate him from many of his colleagues at Caltech.

it offered him the chance to visit more with Einstein. Einstein's repugnance for the bomb and passion for peace were coupled with an ability to speak from the heart that had a great effect on Pauling's own approach to the atomic issue.

But there was an even more important person in Pauling's decision to move toward political action. Ava Helen believed even more strongly than her husband did that citizens had an obligation to speak out where they saw injustice. She had convinced Pauling to join Union Now, an anti-Nazi, pro-democracy group before the war, and had gotten him interested in fighting the internment of Japanese-American citizens during the crisis. Ava Helen, too, felt that the atomic bomb was the most important issue of the day. She was always at Pauling's side during his meetings with Einstein and in the front row at his public talks, encouraging him, critiquing his speeches, urging him to ever greater involvement.

With her help, Pauling became a powerful and popular speaker. His years of teaching had given him the ability to clearly explain technical matters. Through 1946 he made speeches about the physics and technology of the bomb to business clubs and women's associations, high school assemblies and scientific organizations. Later he began adding political content, talking about the insanity of atomic war and the need for world government. In 1946 he and Ava Helen began joining nonscientific political groups that advocated worldwide cooperation and open communication with all other nations, including the Soviet Union.

For a year after the war's end, Pauling's views were not unusual. The FAS succeeded in convincing Congress to take the oversight of atomic energy away from the military and give it to a civilian agency, the Atomic Energy Commission. In 1945 the United Nations was formed—a first step, some thought, toward world government. For a while, President Harry Truman and his advisors openly talked about sharing atomic secrets with other nations, including the Soviet Union.

In the fall of 1946, however, things began to change. The Russian leader Joseph Stalin sealed off Eastern Europe, brutally suppressing democracy there and forcing those nations to adopt communism as their political system, drawing closed what British prime minister Winston Churchill called the Iron Curtain. In China, communist rebels began threatening the government. Alarmed by the rising tide of worldwide communism, U.S. voters began electing anticommunist politicians who rejected the idea of world government, encouraged a tough line with the Soviet Union, and pushed for a build-up of atomic weapons. By late 1947 all talk of sharing bomb technology ceased, and soon anyone who spoke in favor of world government or cooperating with the communists was suspected of actually being a communist. It was the beginning of a long period of silence and fear in America. It was the beginning of the cold war.

During these years Pauling made political speeches because he felt he should, but he continued his scientific work because he loved it. His work with antibodies had confirmed for him the simple but powerful idea that much of the specific activity of biomolecules in the body could be explained through the close fitting of large molecules. Shape and structure were everything—precise, hand-in-glove fitting of molecule to molecule—which he called "detailed molecular complementarity."

He now felt confident that the idea of these close-fitting, complementary shapes was sufficient to explain how antibodies latched onto their target molecules. His own research had shown that the preciseness of the fit between antibody and antigen was incredibly exact, so that even a single atom out of place could significantly loosen the attachment. And he felt that the same could be true of other biological molecules. Through the late 1940s, in a series of brilliant lectures, Pauling outlined the case for complementarity as the core principle of molecular biology. This matching of shape to complementary shape, he said, could explain everything from an enzyme's specificity for a certain substrate to the nose's ability to distinguish between different smells (the theory being that only certain-shaped odor molecules would fit specific odor receptors).

Complementarity could even, Pauling believed, explain the greatest mystery in biology: how living organisms replicated themselves. By now it was known that small units of inheritance called genes carried the instructions for new generations, but their chemical nature was entirely unknown. Pauling, like most scientists, believed that genes were most likely made of proteins.

But how could genes make the precise copies of themselves needed to create new cells and new generations? Pauling had a theory: "In general, the use of a gene . . . as a template would lead to the formation of a molecule not with an identical structure, but with a complementary structure," he said in 1948. "It might happen, of course, that a molecule could be at the same time identical with and complementary to the template upon which it is molded. . . . If the structure that serves as the template (the gene or virus molecule) consists of, say, two parts, which are themselves complementary in structure, then each of these parts can serve as the mold for the production of a replica of the other part, and the complex of two complementary parts can thus serve as the mold for the production of duplicates of itself." This was a fair description of the DNA molecule—four years before its structure was discovered.

Pauling felt he was on the right track, but he refrained from publishing his ideas because he had no proof to present. No one knew for certain what genes were made of, much less how they were shaped, nor had anyone even a crude idea of the detailed structure of any of the proteins. Pauling, intent on solving this last problem, wanted to become the first to publish the precise structure of a protein, and he had a good candidate for the task: keratin.

Keratin, a common protein, is the stuff of hair, fingernails, and animal horn. A good deal of X-ray work had been done on keratin in England, where it was found that hair is made of very long molecules with a structure that repeats itself every 510 picometers along its length. (A picometer is one-trillionth of a meter; for comparison, 100 picometers is roughly the distance from a hydrogen atom to an oxygen atom in a water molecule.) Most of England's leading researchers, and Pauling as well, thought the X-ray data indicated that keratin had some sort of kinked, zigzag structure that accounted for hair's ability to stretch when wet as the molecular kinks straightened out and then shrink back when dry. The 510 picometers were thought to be the distance between each kink.

Using what his lab had discovered about the structure of amino acids and the nature of the peptide bond, and adding in his ideas about hydrogen bonds, Pauling set about building a mental model of keratin. But nothing he tried in the form of a kinked ribbon seemed to work. He could not devise any reasonable structure that obeyed the rules he set himself—especially the rigid peptide bond—and also matched the X-ray data.

Then, during a long visit to England in early 1948, Pauling heard about another approach. British researchers were saying that, instead of a kinked ribbon, keratin and other proteins might have a molecular structure more like a spiral or, as some called it, a helix.

Shortly after learning this, the damp English weather put Pauling to bed in his damp London flat with a severe sinus infection. "The first day I read detective stories and just tried to keep from feeling miserable, and the second day, too," he later remembered. "But I got bored with that, so I thought, 'Why don't I think about the structure of proteins?'" Gathering paper, a ruler, and a pencil, he began sketching out a string of amino acids, measuring to make the proportions as precise as he could, marking the peptide bond with double-thick lines to indicate where the atoms were held rigidly in place. He organized the amino acids so that any side chains would point outward, away from the center of the molecule.

Then Pauling started folding the paper so that the amino acid chain formed a spiral. In a few moments, much to his surprise, he came up with a structure that maintained his planar peptide bond, had reasonable angles for other connections, and easily formed hydrogen bonds between each rise in the spiral. "Well, I forgot all about having a cold then, I was so pleased," he said.

Pleased, that is, until he took out his ruler to measure the distance between each rise of the spiral. It would take months of careful model building to try to confirm the point, but even without that it appeared that the distance between one turn of the chain and the next above it was not close to the 510-picometer repeat found in the X-ray data. There was no way Pauling could see to stretch or compress his model to make it fit. Clearly, something was wrong.

He went back to bed. Pauling told no one about his doodles, filing them away for further study when he returned to California. For the moment, he felt, all he had was "just a piece of paper."

And he went on to other things. When asked once how he had so many good ideas, Pauling answered, "I have a lot of ideas and throw away the bad ones." His fertile mind continued to generate a variety of new ideas through the late 1940s. Some he pursued on his own—protein structure, the nature of the chemical bond in metals, the quantum states of oxygen, a continuing interest in antibodies, the writing of highly influential textbooks for college students—but most he continued to jot down for his research assistants, postdoctoral fellows, and graduate students to follow up.

One of these seemingly offhand ideas turned into an extraordinary advance for medicine. Toward the end of the war, Pauling had been asked to join a committee charged with outlining the postwar funding needs of U.S. medical research. At a committee dinner one night, the talk turned to a rare blood disorder called sickle-cell anemia. One of the members, a physician expert in the disease, described how the red blood cells in these patients were twisted into sickle shapes instead of flat discs. This distortion clogged small blood vessels in the body. The result was joint pain, blood clots, and often death. The disease particularly affected black Americans, this physician said, and there was one more unusual thing: The sickled cells seemed to appear more often in blood in the veins, returning to the lungs, than in the more oxygenated blood found in arteries.

Pauling knew that red blood cells were essentially tiny bags stuffed with hemoglobin. If the cells were sickling, it was likely that hemoglobin was somehow involved. What if the hemoglobin molecules were altered in sickle-cell patients in a way that caused them to stick to each other, clumping up and distorting the cell? This could happen if the surface shape was altered even a little, just enough to create an area complementary to a neighboring hemoglobin. If that happened, the molecules would stick together like an antibody sticks to its antigen. He knew, too, that when oxygen bound to hemoglobin it changed the molecule's shape, perhaps enough to reduce the "stickiness" and lower the amount of sickling.

This was an idea that perhaps could have occurred only to Pauling, but to prove it he would have to find differences in structure between normal and sickle-cell hemoglobin. He gave that job to Harvey Itano, a young physician who was earning his Ph.D. under Pauling. Itano, joined later by a postdoctoral fellow, John Singer, worked for a year trying to find the structural difference Pauling had predicted, but they could not find anything. The hemoglobins were the same size, same general shape, and had the same reactions to tests; in short, they appeared to be identical.

But Itano and Singer kept at it. Finally, while Pauling was in England, they put the hemoglobins through an extremely sensitive new technique called electrophoresis, which separates proteins by the electrical charges on their surfaces. And here they found their answer: The sickle-cell hemoglobin carried a few more positively charged atoms on its surface. The difference was not great, but there was in fact a structural difference.

This was astounding—a slight change in the electrical charge of a single molecule in the body meant the difference between a healthy human and one with a deadly disease. Never before had the cause of a disease been traced to an alteration in a single molecule, and this discovery—

Pauling called it history's first "molecular disease"—caused an international sensation. Itano and Singer's follow-up work demonstrated a pattern of genetic inheritance for the disease and added to its importance as one of the cornerstone discoveries in modern medicine.

By the end of the 1940s, there seemed no scientific height that Pauling could not scale. There was talk of a Nobel Prize after the sickle-cell discovery in the late 1940s. In England he was awarded honorary degrees from that nation's three major universities—Cambridge, Oxford, and London—the first American, he was told, ever so honored. At home he was nominated for the presidency of the National Academy of Sciences and elected president

Pauling and his assistant, Robert Corey, with a model of a molecule.

of the American Chemical Society. But still the greatest prize eluded Pauling: to discover the precise structure of a protein.

After his return from England, in the winter of 1948, Pauling quietly assigned a visiting professor of physics named Herman Branson the job of rechecking his idea about keratin helixes. The instructions he provided Branson were somewhat open-ended. Ignore the X-ray data for the moment, he directed, but use the limiting factors of known amino acids' dimensions and the planar peptide bond, and look for structures that maximize hydrogen bonding to pin the helix in position. Given those limits, how many stable helixes could be devised? After a year's work, Branson came up with just two, one being the same that Pauling had sketched in England. He gave Pauling detailed calculations for the parameters of both—one more tightly wound, called the alpha helix, and a looser one, the gamma helix—and went on to other research.

Again Pauling was confounded. Neither of Branson's two stable helixes matched the 510-picometer repeated distance along the axis that the X-ray data said should be there. The tighter spiral came close, at 540 picometers, but not close enough.

And again he hesitated to publish the findings. "I felt so strongly that the structure must explain the X-ray data that I took a chance by waiting," he remembered. Perhaps, he was beginning to think, it would take 50 years of work to solve protein's structure after all. Pauling let it sit for a year until he was jolted into action by a scientific paper published by Sir William Bragg, the X-ray pioneer, whom Pauling had beaten to the structure of silicates 20 years before, and his research group at the Cavendish Laboratory in Cambridge. Pauling had visited there, finding it a place where protein research was both well-funded and surprisingly advanced. If anyone had a shot at beating Pauling to the structure of keratin, it was Bragg's group. The somewhat unfocused paper by Bragg that Pauling read in 1950 was all about protein structures. But because the British did not pay enough attention to the idea of a rigid peptide bond, which Pauling believed to be absolutely necessary, they twisted and bent their theoretical structures in ways he believed impossible. No wonder Bragg's group concluded that none of the 20 kinked chains and spirals they proposed was quite right.

One of their forms, however, came very close to Pauling and Branson's alpha helix, a near miss that was enough to get Pauling back in the game. Feeling forced into action by the British advances, Pauling decided to ignore the contradictory X-ray evidence and publish his ideas anyway. He and his assistant Robert Corey, an expert in the painstakingly precise art of interpreting X-ray crystallography data from proteins, wrote a short note in the fall of 1950 outlining their two spirals. Then Pauling and Corey threw themselves into the hard labor of pinning down the position of every atom in their models.

They were aided by some unexpected good news. A British manufacturer of artificial fibers announced that it had created synthetic protein strands very much like keratin by joining glycine amino acids with peptide bonds. This artificial protein formed itself into a spiral with roughly the dimensions Pauling predicted for his alpha helix. That was encouraging. But even better was the news that the X-ray pattern from this synthetic protein did *not* show the 510-picometer repeat found in natural keratin. Pauling was very excited by this result. Perhaps the confounded X-ray data had nothing to do with the essential spiral structure at all but was simply an artifact of how the spirals interacted with each other in natural proteins.

Pauling and Corey worked feverishly now, expanding their ideas beyond the two helixes to additional structures for silk that they called pleated sheets. They also explored more complex structures for the proteins in feathers, muscle, and collagen, a common protein found in bone, cartilage, and tendon.

On February 28, 1951, his 50th birthday, Pauling sent to press an extremely detailed complete description of the two helixes he and Corey had started with. He then spent the following weeks working on his other structures. "I am having a hard time keeping my feet on the ground now," he wrote a former student, "I have been working night and day, neglecting almost everything else."

The result was one of the most extraordinary sets of papers in 20th-century science. Seven appeared together, dominating the May 1951 issue of the *Proceedings of the National Academy of Sciences*. There was a detailed description of the pleated sheet for silk. There was a new model for the protein in feathers, and new ideas about the structure of artificial proteins, globular proteins, and muscle.

The May 1951 issue of the Proceedings of the National Academy of Sciences was dominated by several revolutionary articles by Pauling on the structure of proteins.

THE STRUCTURE OF PROTEINS: TWO HYDROGEN-BONDED HELICAL CONFIGURATIONS OF THE POLYPEPTIDE CHAIN

BY LINUS PAULING, ROBERT B. COREY, AND H. R. BRANSON*

GATES AND CRELLIN LABORATORIES OF CHEMISTRY,
CALIFORNIA INSTITUTE OF TECHNOLOGY, PASADENA, CALIFORNIA†

Communicated February 28, 1951

During the past fifteen years we have been attacking the problem of the structure of proteins in several ways. One of these ways is the complete and accurate determination of the crystal structure of amino acids, peptides, and other simple substances related to proteins, in order that information about interatomic distances, bond angles, and other configurational parameters might be obtained that would permit the reliable prediction of reasonable configurations for the polypeptide chain. We have now used this information to construct two reasonable hydrogen-bonded helical configurations for the polypeptide chain; we think that it is likely that these configurations constitute an important part of the structure of both fibrous and globular proteins, as well as of synthetic polypeptides. A letter announcing their discovery was published last year.[1]

The problem that we have set ourselves is that of finding all hydrogen-bonded structures for a single polypeptide chain, in which the residues are

There was what Pauling called an "astounding structure" for collagen, a complex of three of his alpha helixes wound around each other to form a cable.

Taken together, Pauling's protein papers constituted an amazing event, a leap from knowing nothing about the detailed structure of any protein to knowing a great deal about many of them. It raised the stakes for protein researchers worldwide, who now had to detail their structures to the level of precisely placing each atom if they wanted to match Pauling.

Not everything in these papers was correct, of course. It was later proved that Pauling and Corey's ideas about several proteins, including collagen and muscle, were wrong, and others needed refining. The looser, gamma, helix was never found to be important in nature.

But none of this could eclipse Pauling's towering achievement. His alpha helix was soon confirmed to be the structure of keratin and was found as well to be an important component of many other proteins of widely varying types. By using his wits, his model building, and his belief in the rules of chemistry, Pauling had succeeded in jumping to an understanding of the correct structure for a protein years before anyone else might have.

And yet Pauling had not solved the mystery of life. His alpha helix was an important structural feature of many proteins, but it could not explain how the important ones worked. Apart from hair and horn, Pauling's alpha helix seemed to explain nothing about protein activity. To make an antibody, for instance, sections of alpha helix would have to bend and twist to create an area complementary in shape to the target molecule. Pauling's model did not account for bends, nor did it predict in any way how the alpha helix could create the fantastic variety of shapes necessary for proteins.

At the same time, it was becoming clear that the real chemical secret of life—the stuff that made genes—was not

text continues on page 95

Until the early 1950s, most scientists, including Linus Pauling, believed that protein—not nucleic acid—was the stuff that genes were made of. It took a kitchen blender to convince them otherwise.

Researchers knew that genes were hidden in the chromosomes, which themselves were composed of nucleoprotein, a tangled mixture of proteins and nucleic acids. But most thought that only the protein parts of the chromosomes were important. Only protein was thought to have the complexity necessary for determining the growth of an organism. Proteins, after all, were made of 20 or more different amino acids. The nucleic acids, made of just four building blocks called nucleotides, probably existed only to support the proteins.

Opinions did not change even when Oswald Avery, an American medical researcher, discovered in 1944 that DNA could by itself transfer genetic traits from one *Pneumococcus* bacterium to another. Pauling knew Avery and his work, but he did not accept the evidence. "I was so pleased with proteins, you know, that I thought that proteins probably are the hereditary material rather than nucleic acids—but that of course nucleic acids played a part," he said. "In whatever I wrote about nucleic acids, I mentioned nucleoproteins, and I was thinking more of the protein than of the nucleic acids."

It took another, more dramatic, set of experiments to kill the idea that genes were made of protein. In 1952, the American microbiologist Alfred Hershey and his colleague Martha Chase labeled bacterial viruses using different radioactive tags for their protein coats and nucleic acid cores. They then allowed the "hot" viruses to infect and replicate inside bacteria, stopping the process at specific stages and separating the viruses from the bacteria by whipping everything in a kitchen blender. By tracking the radioactive tags, they discovered that the viral protein remained outside the bacteria, doing nothing. The DNA from the viruses, on the other hand, was injected into the bacteria and showed up in viral offspring. Therefore, DNA alone was involved in replication.

As soon as he learned about the Hershey-Chase experiments at a scientific meeting in France in the summer of 1952, Pauling realized that the protein gene was a myth. He immediately switched his attention to DNA and started a new, and very fast, attack on its structure.

text continued from page 93

protein at all. After a decisive set of experiments by the American microbiologists Alfred Hershey and Martha Chase, completed in early 1952, it became clear that genes were made of a long-chain molecule called deoxyribonucleic acid, or DNA.

Pauling was still refining his protein models, altering the alpha helix to allow for turns, and proposing that the 510-picometer repeat in natural keratin resulted from a supercoiling of the long alpha helix molecule itself, like a piece of yarn wound around a finger. But he also became interested in DNA. Compared to proteins, he thought it would be a relatively simple problem. Instead of the 20 amino acids that went into proteins, DNA was made up of only four subunits, called nucleotides, each consisting of a sugar attached to a phosphate group and a large, flat carbon-and-nitrogen ring structure called a base. There had not been any very good X-ray studies of DNA published, but the fuzzy few that there were seemed to indicate that the DNA molecule was probably a helix.

With this in mind, in the fall of 1952 Pauling made a fast attack on the structure of DNA. He started by looking first at what little was known of the structure of the subunits (unfortunately, no one had completed a good analysis of the size and shape of any nucleotide), then considering which rules of chemistry applied to this type of molecule. Again unfortunately, there was no peptide bond-like clue here either. And he got off on the wrong foot by overestimating DNA's density, leading him to think it might be made of three chains wrapped tightly around one another.

With poor basic information, and operating with the wrong density for DNA, Pauling next thought about the simplest way to make a regularly repeating structure. Just as he had pointed the amino acid side chains away from the center of the alpha helix, thus simplifying the problem of how to fit things into the middle of the molecule, he now pointed the flat DNA bases to the outside of his proposed structures, where they too would be out of the way. Having the bases pointed out meant that the phosphates would be packed tightly together at the DNA core, in the middle of the three intertwined chains. After a few days' work with pencil, ruler, and paper, Pauling had sketched a rough structure that seemed to match the available data. It was very tightly wrapped, but that was good in a way, because nature preferred a tight fit at the biomolecular level, so that fewer small molecules or ions could get inside and throw things off.

Pauling now felt he was on the verge of another great discovery. The only problem came at the core, where the phosphates were packed together so tightly that they were jostling one another. When Corey checked out Pauling's calculations in more detail, he reported back the disappointing news that there was no way the phosphates could fit as Pauling was proposing. For weeks, Pauling stretched and twisted and distorted his model as much as he felt he reasonably could. Finally he made the phosphates fit.

And he decided to publish. Only a month had passed since he had first sat down to take a serious look at the structure of DNA. There were still many questions to answer, such as why the phosphates, which would probably carry a negative charge, wouldn't repel each other and blow the structure apart. Pauling decided to ignore this question for the moment, as he had ignored the 510 picometer repeat with the alpha helix.

He had been right with the alpha helix, and he felt confident enough in himself to ignore the niggling problems about DNA as well. If his proposed DNA structure were right, the reasons for the odd phosphate behavior could be found later. Perhaps there were positive ions in the center of the molecule. Or there might be something unique to the physiology of chromosomes that altered phosphate chemistry. Pauling was willing to ignore the smaller questions as long as his major structure looked right.

And there was an additional reason to hurry. Pauling's second son, Peter, now a graduate student in the Cavendish Laboratory, was working with a couple of men who were also trying to crack the structure of DNA. Peter wrote his father about them: Jim Watson, a tall, thin, American post-doctoral fellow, and Francis Crick, an older British graduate student with a quick mind and a love of chatter. They were all part of Sir William Bragg's group, the ones Pauling had beaten twice, most recently to the structure of the alpha helix. Pauling did not think a postdoc and a grad student represented serious competition, but the structure of DNA was a great prize. He did not want to be the second to discover it.

So, at the end of December 1952, he and Corey sent in their article on DNA structure for publication in the *Proceedings of the National Academy of Sciences*. It would prove the greatest blunder Linus Pauling would ever make.

When Peter Pauling showed Watson and Crick a pre-publication draft of his father's DNA paper, they could not believe what they saw. As fans of Linus Pauling's, they had carefully imitated his techniques of model building and chemical rule making in their own attack on DNA. They, too, had considered a three-stranded structure a few months earlier, but had been lucky enough to show it to Rosalind Franklin, an x-ray crystallographer at nearby King's College, who had recently taken the world's best X-ray pictures of DNA. She tore it apart.

Not only have you got all those negatively charged phosphates in the middle, she said, but your molecule is too dense. Her own studies had shown that in the body, DNA soaked up a great deal of water, too much to be accounted for by the three-stranded model. She was convinced that DNA existed in two forms, one "dry" and more dense, the other "wet" and fully extended. The phosphates need to be on the outside, she said, where they could be encased in water. She eventually showed Watson and Crick her X-ray photos of the pure "wet" form of DNA, which put them on the right track.

Now, looking at Pauling's paper, Watson and Crick were ecstatic. The master of structural chemistry had made an elementary mistake by putting his phosphates at the core. The density was wrong, and the negative phosphates would repel each other. There was still a chance for them to interpret the structure first. Crick wrote Pauling a short, acidic note in response to his paper, noting dryly, "We were very struck by the ingenuity of the structure. The only doubt I have is that I do not see what holds it together."

Then he and Watson went back to work. Within a few months, the two of them pulled off the scientific coup of the century, coming up with a new DNA structure made of two complementary chains wound around each other to form a spiral—they called it a double helix—each of which, when separated, could form another, identical chain. This was exactly what Pauling had described as a likely feature of the genetic material four years earlier.

Within a few weeks of reading Watson and Crick's description of their model, Pauling graciously agreed that it looked as if they had gotten it right. He continued thinking about DNA—correcting the Watson and Crick structure on one point involving a hydrogen bond—and encouraged workers in his laboratories to do DNA research. Throughout, he maintained his sense of humor. When Alex Rich, one of the researchers in Pauling's group, was later making progress in his own DNA studies, Pauling stuck his head into the office and said, "You work hard on that problem, Alex. I like *most* of the important discoveries to be made in Pasadena."

Getting DNA wrong—very publicly—was, however, a blow to Pauling's pride, and an error he would regret for the rest of his life. Watson and Crick would go on to win the Nobel Prize for their discovery, and work on DNA and its biological function would dominate the life sciences for the next fifty years. Pauling would never play a significant role in it.

And rarely would a year go by after that without some journalist asking Pauling where he had gone wrong. Sometimes he said it was the incorrect density data. Sometimes he suggested that it was muddy X-ray photos. Ava Helen finally tired of hearing the excuses and cut through them all with a simple question: "If that was such an important problem," she asked, "why didn't you work harder on it?"

Pauling, surrounded by molecular models, in his Caltech office around 1957.

The Price of Peace

Although he handled it gracefully, Linus Pauling was deeply chagrined by his DNA failure. His public embarrassment had a permanent effect: After 1953, he made no further attempts to solve the configuration of any large biomolecule. Apart from some clean-up work with proteins, Pauling gave up the quest that had engaged him for 20 years and began looking for something new.

In the meantime, he refocused his attention on the political arena. He had maintained his antibomb activism through the late 1940s even as the cold war deepened and anticommunist fervor created an atmosphere of distrust and political repression in the United States. As Albert Einstein and other scientists had predicted, in late 1949 the Soviet Union developed its own atomic bomb. At the same time, Mao Zedong's rebels triumphed in China, bringing the world's most populous nation under communist control. Then, in the summer of 1950, communist North Korea invaded South Korea, setting off the Korean War, a bloody conflict that cost the lives of thousands of U.S. troops.

Most Americans believed that a gigantic communist conspiracy was under way to conquer the world, and the presence of huge Russian and Chinese Communist armies in Europe and Asia that overwhelmingly outnumbered those of the U.S. and its allies made it clear to Western leaders that America would be defenseless without atomic bombs. Only a shield of nuclear weapons, the thinking went, would deter the communists from sweeping over us. Anyone who questioned the making of more and more powerful bombs was thus seen at best as a communist dupe or "fellow traveler" and at worst as a traitor.

To root out communist spies and lessen dissent at home, loyalty programs were initiated in which government employees, from soldiers to schoolteachers, were required to swear they were not members of the Communist party. Investigative boards scrutinized people's membership in suspect political groups. Opportunistic politicians used state and congressional committees to investigate suspected communists in government and private enterprise. Newspapers, magazines, and radio commentators joined the hunt for "Reds." The costs of being named a communist or communist-supporting "fellow traveler" were, for great numbers of Americans, a ruined reputation, a lost job, and even, if they refused to cooperate with investigators, prison.

In this atmosphere of repression, many whose politics were liberal, who favored international cooperation and domestic political freedom, fell silent. Membership in the Federation of American Scientists and other liberal political action groups dwindled. The Emergency Committee of Atomic Scientists disbanded. The left wing in American politics crumbled. It was simply too dangerous to criticize American policy.

But Pauling, at the urging of his conscience and his wife, continued to speak out—and suffered for it. The FBI investigated him for years to see if he was a Communist party member (he was not). Agents combed through his personnel files at Caltech, questioned his friends and coworkers, and researched his activities in such groups as the FAS and the Progressive Citizens of America. He was called before government boards, asked to explain his actions, and publicly accused of being a communist. He was refused security clearance to oversee classified national defense projects, stripped of federal research grants, and repeatedly denied a passport to travel outside the United States. He was vilified in the press.

Still Pauling refused to cut back on his speeches. He signed petitions against loyalty programs, argued for the free right to travel, supported those who had been fired because of their politics, and refused to resign from groups the government designated "Communist fronts." He believed it his right as an American to speak his mind freely and his duty as a scientist to encourage people to reach their own conclusions, free from government interference. "You must always search for truth," he told a group of college students. "Truth does not depend upon the point of view. If your neighbor does not see things as you do, then you must search for the truth. If a statement is made in one country but not another, then you must search for the truth."

By 1950, Pauling's search for truth had branded him a leading fellow traveler. Many of his former friends at Caltech now began to look away when they passed him on the street. A pharmaceutical company that had paid him to be a consultant suddenly dropped him from its payroll. Lee DuBridge, the president of Caltech, asked Pauling to cut back on his political speeches, because conservative donors were refusing to give money to the school until Caltech got rid of "that Communist." When Pauling refused, Caltech launched its own internal probe of his political activities to see if there were grounds for firing him.

Finally, even for Pauling, the pressure became too great. In 1951 he stopped making speeches critical of U.S. defense policies, quit several of the most controversial organizations he had joined, and for two years devoted himself to protein and DNA work. But his self-imposed silence did not seem to help. He continued to be targeted by the press and harassed by the government. When he requested a passport it was sometimes denied, and even if one was granted, for a limited time, his every move outside the United States was tracked by government officials and military officers. His name still appeared in published lists of suspected communists. Congressional investigative groups such as the House Un-American Activities Committee still pointed him out publicly as a supposed threat to American security.

Then, on March 1, 1954, the United States tested a new kind of bomb, a "superbomb" powerful enough to obliterate an entire Pacific island. Pauling was outraged as he learned more about it over the following weeks. It appeared to be a thousand times more powerful than the bomb used on Hiroshima. The one blast that destroyed Bikini Atoll contained more explosive force than all the bombs used in every war in human history to that time.

This was shocking enough. But there was another, even more dangerous effect of the new bomb. It was so strong that it punched a hole through the lower levels of the atmosphere and spewed radioactive dust high into the stratosphere. There the radiation stayed aloft for weeks, slowly circling the globe. As it fell back to earth, scientists began to study it, and many became frightened.

This radiation, which scientists called fallout, was full of new and strange radioactive substances, some never seen on earth before. Anyone exposed to high levels of fallout could suffer radiation poisoning, as did the unlucky crew of a Japanese fishing boat 90 miles away from the Bikini blast— nausea and fever, burned skin, bleeding gums, hair coming out in clumps, death if the exposure was great enough. No one knew what low-level exposure to fallout might do. Most of the world's population, however, was now being forced to find out.

The threat of the new superbomb brought Pauling back into the political arena. He began searching for the

text continues on page 106

I n 1951, at the height of anticommunist repression in the United States, a military review board demanded that Pauling explain his political views. The board's aim was to determine his fitness to review the classified government documents that were sometimes involved in Caltech grant requests.

Pauling replied with a long statement in which he made a scientific case for free speech. The way he saw it, American politics could be thought of as a matter of statistics: "The principle upon which a true democratic system operates is that no single man is wise enough to make the correct decisions about the very complex problems that arise, and that the correct decisions are to be made by the process of averaging the opinions of all the citizens in a democracy. These opinions will correspond to a probability distribution curve extending from far on the left to far on the right. If, now, we say that all of the opinions that extend too far to the right . . . are abnormal, and are to be excluded in taking the average, then the average that we obtain will be the wrong one. And an understanding of the laws of probability would accordingly make it evident to the citizen that the operation of the democratic system requires that everyone have the right to express his opinions about political questions, no matter what that opinion might be."

Pauling was pointing out that no good scientist would lop off just one end of a set of findings, because the resulting average would be thrown off. In America, the attempt to lop off the views of those on the left wing of the political spectrum would have the same skewing effect—and so he concluded that the best system, the most scientific, democratic system, would be to allow free speech for all.

text continued from page 104

truth about fallout, and started telling the world what he found.

And the world listened. Now in his mid–50s, Pauling was the world's foremost chemist. His ideas about the chemical bond had revolutionized the field; his chemistry textbooks were among the most popular and influential ever written; his ideas about protein structure and molecular disease had made history. He had been awarded honorary doctorates by the world's greatest universities and had won almost every significant honor available to chemists.

One great honor, however, had eluded him: the Nobel Prize. For years his colleagues and students had wondered why the prize was given to other, less prolific chemists—even, in 1951, to one of Pauling's former students—while the great man himself was overlooked. Pauling reasoned that he had been ignored because Alfred Nobel's will said specifically that the prizes were to be given for a single important discovery. Pauling instead had reshaped all of chemistry, creating an entire body of work, an edifice of structural chemistry composed of many parts. "That was the trouble," as he said. "What was the single great discovery I had made?"

So it came as a wonderful surprise when, on the afternoon of November 3, 1954, Pauling received a phone call from a newspaper reporter. "What is your reaction to winning the Nobel Prize in chemistry?" the reporter asked. Pauling asked what it was for. "Chemistry," the reporter replied. "No, what does the citation say?" Pauling wanted to know which of his many discoveries was being honored. "For research into the nature of the chemical bond," the reporter read, "and its application to the elucidation of complex substances." Pauling gave a wide grin. The Nobel was being given him for everything he had done in chemistry from 1928 to his work with the alpha helix. The Nobel officials had given him a lifetime award.

Winning the Nobel helped lift the clouds of suspicion that surrounded him at Caltech. He received hundreds of

letters and telegrams from wellwishers, attended many parties in his honor, and was glad when old friends who had
avoided him now clapped him on the back and gave him
their congratulations.

Just before he left to receive his prize in Stockholm, the
entire Caltech community threw him a lavish party with a
catered dinner, speeches in his honor, and a hilarious series
of skits and songs called "The Road to Stockholm," put
together by his students and fellow faculty members. In one
particularly funny sketch, Ava Helen was portrayed as a
lovesick student singing to her teacher:

> Dr. Linus Pauling is the man for me.
> He makes violent changes in my chemistry.
> Oh fie, when he rolls his eyes
> All my atoms ionize.
> When he's near blood molecules rush to my face,
> And I couldn't tell an acid from first base.
> Oh joy, you'll never see
> Such affinity.

It was a joyous evening, full of warmth and laughter and
generous high spirits. Pauling's happiness continued through
the frosty days of early December, when he and his family
arrived in Sweden to receive the Nobel. The U.S. Department
of State, faced with the possibility of an international outcry if
Pauling was again refused a passport, had reluctantly granted
him the right to travel. He arrived to wide public acclaim in
Scandinavia as a man who was not only a great researcher but
a person of moral conviction whose voice would not be
stilled. The Nobel ceremony itself, "one of the most impres-
sive . . . held in the modern world," Pauling said, was held
in the ornate Stockholm Concert Hall, where Sweden's
King Gustavus VI handed Pauling the gold Nobel medal.

Afterward, Pauling was asked to give an address to a
crowd of hundreds of cheering Swedish university students
who had come to acclaim the new Nobelists. His words
were reprinted in all the papers in the nation: "Perhaps as

A beaming Linus Pauling is surrounded by his family after receiving the Nobel Prize for chemistry in 1954.

one of the older generation, I should preach a little sermon to you, but I do not propose to do so. I shall, instead, give you a word of advice about how to behave toward your elders," he said, his voice ringing clearly across the crowded square. "When an old and distinguished person speaks to you, listen to him carefully and with respect—*but do not believe him*. Never put your trust in anything but your own intellect. Your elder, no matter whether he has gray hair or has lost his hair, no matter whether he is a Nobel laureate, may be wrong. . . . So you must always be skeptical—*always think for yourself*." The students cheered wildly.

After the ceremonies, the Paulings embarked on a triumphant four-month world tour, making stops and delivering political and scientific speeches in Israel, India (where they shared dinner with Prime Minister Nehru), Thailand, and Japan. The Japanese, whose long-standing concern over atomic weapons had been raised to new heights by the superbomb fallout, especially appreciated Pauling's heroic work against the development of nuclear weapons, and he was mobbed wherever he went. Japanese scientists were leading the world in the analysis of fallout, and as he talked with them Pauling grew more worried about how low levels of radiation exposure might affect human health.

He returned to America refreshed and reinvigorated. For six months, from the time his Nobel had been announced until he returned to Pasadena, Pauling had been honored and fêted, applauded and attended. He had dined with kings and prime ministers. He had delivered more than 50 antibomb talks to enthusiastic audiences. And he had learned that his concerns—about fallout, the arms race, the cold war—were shared by the world. He returned home in 1955 secure in his beliefs and ready to continue his fight against the superbomb.

Through the late 1950s, Pauling still dabbled in science. He remained interested in the medical applications of his work and wrote pieces about sickle-cell anemia and the role of abnormal molecules in human disease. He toyed with the idea that perhaps misshapen molecules were the cause of mental diseases. But he had lost the passion and focus that had marked his earlier work.

In general, Pauling turned away from research and devoted most of his time to the antibomb movement. As Caltech's president, Lee DuBridge, put it, "For a while there he lost touch with science." Pauling's prime worry was fallout and the health effects of small increases in radiation exposure. Although U.S. government officials tried their best to reassure the public that fallout posed no danger, Pauling thought the scientific data indicated otherwise. There was in fact a growing body of evidence indicating that low-level radiation could damage the DNA in cells and cause mutations and disease.

Humans were exposed to naturally occurring "background radiation" of course, from sunlight, cosmic rays, and the decay of naturally occurring radioactive elements. Pauling agreed with most geneticists of the day that this background radiation caused a constant low level of disease and mutation.

And he agreed with the government that the testing of nuclear bombs through 1955 had increased the total background level of radiation by only about 1 percent. But he differed in interpreting what that small increase meant. Spokespeople for the Atomic Energy Commission said it was negligible for any individual, equivalent to the increase caused by wearing a watch with a radium dial or moving from sea level to Denver, where the higher altitude meant greater exposure to cosmic rays.

However, Pauling looked at the same numbers in a different way. Instead of calculating the increased risk to individuals, he used entire populations. If all of the 1.5 million birth defects around the world each year were caused by background radiation, he argued, then a 1 percent increase translated into an additional 15,000 defective babies each year, all caused by bomb testing. A minuscule increase in one individual's risk of cancer could look like a significant worldwide health problem when analyzed in this way. By extrapolating these population-based figures over many generations, in Pauling's analysis fallout began to look like a very serious health problem indeed.

Pauling took every opportunity to make his views public, speaking widely and publishing wherever he could. But it was a battle fought in the fog—both sides in the fallout debate were using sketchy data. And, as it was eventually shown, both were essentially correct in their estimates. It was simply a matter of how the estimates were framed. As Pauling said, "There is considerable uncertainty about estimated values in this field. But I think that we should consider the worst possible case rather than the best possible case."

Pauling's approach proved the more compelling. People began to listen seriously to his estimates. His case was made even stronger when it was found that fallout included strontium 90, a long-lived radioactive species with an unfortunate chemical similarity to calcium. Researchers found that when strontium 90 fell to earth, it could be ingested by cattle and passed through their milk to humans, where it was deposited in bones. The growing bones of children were especially affected. Once in the bones, strontium 90 exposed the surrounding tissue to radiation. Pauling and other antibomb activists used the issue to sharply etch an image of radiation-poisoned children's milk in the minds of millions of families.

As the fallout debate heated up, so did the arms race. Soviet scientists rushed to create their own superbomb, and both sides felt compelled to test more and more weapons of ever-increasing power. As they did, more and more radioactive fallout spread around the world.

By 1957, thanks in part to Pauling's ceaseless warnings and the work of other activists and antibomb organizations, public opinion began to shift decisively toward stopping all testing of nuclear weapons. But this was not enough. Pauling wanted to show the world that many of the men and women who understood most intimately the dangers of nuclear fallout—the scientists—believed it should be stopped. Scientists had traditionally been silent on public issues, preferring instead to concentrate on their research. But Pauling felt that if they were simply asked to sign their names to a statement about the issue, they might make their feelings known. Accordingly, in 1957 he wrote and sent to thousands of American scientists a petition asking them to support a ban on all nuclear testing. Much of the mailing was done from the kitchen table of Pauling's Pasadena home, with Ava Helen and some of her friends stuffing envelopes and licking stamps.

The response was astounding. Within two weeks, Pauling got back more than 2,000 signatures, including some from Nobel Prize winners and many members of the National Academy of Sciences. Pauling released his results to the press and announced that he was expanding his petition drive to the entire world scientific community. Within a few months he had gathered 9,000 more signatures. In January 1958 he presented the entire list to the secretary-general of the United Nations.

Pauling's petitions made worldwide news. Scientists had not spoken with this degree of unanimity about a political issue since the days when they fought for civilian control of atomic bomb research just after World War II, and the number of petition signers impressed both the public and political leaders. Surely if these scientists believed that the fallout from nuclear testing was dangerous, then something was wrong with the government's efforts to convince the public that fallout was harmless.

These efforts got Pauling into hot water. He continued to be blasted by government officials and right-wing press columnists as a communist dupe. At Caltech, three members of the board of trustees resigned to protest Pauling's ceaseless antibomb activism. Lee DuBridge, Caltech's president, concerned both about Pauling's political notoriety and his neglect of scientific research, asked him in 1958 to resign as head of the chemistry division. Pauling was stung by the request but agreed to step down, both for the good of the school and to free more of his time for political activism. He was still a faculty member, still taught occasional classes and oversaw a large group of researchers. But the warm feelings that followed his Nobel Prize had evaporated. From this point on, Pauling became increasingly isolated and unhappy at Caltech and began looking for a new position.

But through it all he remained, on the surface, a joyful warrior for peace. Pauling made speech after speech before peace groups. On television he debated Edward Teller, the anticommunist physicist known as the father of the H-bomb, and Atomic Energy Commission scientific advisor Willard Libby. He wrote an antibomb book titled *No More War!* and traveled the world in support of other prominent antibomb leaders, such as the philosopher Bertrand Russell in England

and the Nobel Peace Prize–winning humanitarian physician Albert Schweitzer in Africa. He toured the Soviet Union, speaking to the people there about the need to stop testing bombs. Ava Helen, always by his side, always encouraging, was asked to speak about American women's attitudes toward peace. The Paulings were now true citizens of the world, and their thoughts about the dangers of fallout and the need for world government were reaching an ever-growing audience.

Pauling's speeches often started the same way. "We live in a wonderful world, a beautiful world! I like this world. I like everything in it: the stars, the mountains, the seas, lakes and rivers, the forests, the minerals, the molecules—and especially the human beings," he would say. But all these wonderful things, he continued, were threatened with disaster from nuclear war and bomb-test fallout.

"Why are these weapons of destruction being made? Are those weapons going to be used? Are the leaders of the great nations of the world going to sacrifice all of the people in the world because they are not willing to negotiate in a rational way with one another?" he asked. After painting a picture of the horrors of nuclear war and the deadly effects of fallout, he would ask his audiences to support a new way toward peace. "We need to have the spirit of science in international affairs to find the right solution, the just solution of international problems, not the effort by each nation to get the better of other nations, to do harm to them when possible. . . . The time has now come for morality to take its proper place in the conduct of world affairs; the time has now come for the nations of the world to submit to the just regulation of their conduct by international law."

Everywhere he and Ava Helen went, in North and South America, Europe, Asia, and Australia, Pauling's appeal to reason was heard by enthusiastic crowds. But at home he was still subjected to harassment. In 1960, a Senate investigative subcommittee subpoenaed him to explain how he had gotten so many signatures—especially ones from behind the Iron Curtain—on his test-ban petitions. The subcommittee chairman, Democratic Senator Thomas Dodd, was convinced that Pauling's effort was too big to have been mounted from his home; somehow, he thought, the Communist party must have been involved. Pauling cooperated with the inquiry up to the point when he was asked in a public session to provide the names of those who had helped him distribute his petitions in other nations. Pauling refused. "The circulation of petitions is an important part of our democratic process," he told the subcommittee. "If it is abolished or inhibited, it would be a step toward a police state. No matter what assurances the subcommittee might give me concerning the use of names, I am convinced the names would be used for reprisals against these enthusiastic, idealistic, high-minded workers for peace."

Pauling risked a contempt citation and a prison sentence by refusing to cooperate. But his stand was applauded by newspapers around the world, and when hundreds of letters of support deluged Dodd's office, the subcommittee backed down.

Pauling's antibomb energy seemed ceaseless. He organized a successful international scientific gathering in Oslo, Norway, to bring world attention to the proliferation of nuclear bombs.

He accepted a dinner invitation from President John F. Kennedy in 1961—then picketed the White House the morning before, carrying a sign saying, "Mr. Kennedy . . . We Have No Right to Test." Everything he did was done to attract maximum attention and keep public pressure on the government to discontinue its bomb tests and stop the fallout.

Pauling protests nuclear testing outside the White House on the day before he was to attend a dinner there with President John F. Kennedy.

Finally, in the summer of 1963, after years of wavering, stalled negotiations, and endless hesitation, the government appeared to be close to signing a test-ban treaty with the Soviet Union. President Kennedy had given the effort his full attention, and his negotiators had overcome a final hurdle by agreeing with the Soviets that underground bomb tests, which, after all, released almost no fallout, could continue, as long as there was a ban on testing in the atmosphere. A treaty banning atmospheric tests—the first nuclear treaty in history—was signed on August 5, 1963.

This treaty was not everything the Paulings had hoped for, not a complete ban on weapons development and testing. But it was a major step forward; it would stop the threat of fallout.

The test ban went into effect on October 10. The next morning, as the Paulings were eating breakfast with friends, a call came in from their daughter Linda. "Daddy, have you heard the news?" she asked her father.

"No," Pauling said, "What news?"

Pauling listened, then quietly put down the receiver. He turned to Ava Helen, a look of astonishment on his face. Linda had told him that he had been awarded the Nobel Peace Prize.

7

Vitamin C

Winning the Nobel Peace Prize was a complete and wonderful surprise. The front yard of Pauling's Pasadena home quickly filled with journalists and camera crews. Telegrams of congratulation began arriving by the score. The phone would not stop ringing. Pauling held a short news conference in which he told everyone how proud and happy he was. "I also hope," he said, "that this award will now make it respectable to work for peace in the United States."

Pauling was jubilant. For years he had suffered personal attacks and professional setbacks because of his antibomb efforts. Now he was vindicated. "I gave over five hundred public lectures about radioactive fallout and nuclear war and the need for stopping the bomb tests in the atmosphere and the need for eliminating war ultimately," he later told an interviewer. "I was doing something that I didn't care to do very much, except for reasons of morality and conviction. . . . So when I received word in 1963 that I had been given the Nobel Prize, I felt that showed that the sacrifice that I had made was worthwhile."

The Peace Prize was indeed a signal honor, especially because it made Pauling the first person in history to have

Pauling speaks with reporters in his living room after learning that he had won the Nobel Peace Prize.

won two unshared Nobels. (Marie Curie had also won two, but one of hers was shared with her husband and another physicist.) The public response, however, was not all congratulatory. A number of newspapers and magazines were critical, arguing that President Kennedy was a better choice for the Prize than Pauling, whom the *New York Herald-Tribune* dubbed a "placarding peacenik." *Life* magazine headlined its editorial about the prize "A Weird Insult from Norway," adding that "however distinguished as a chemist, the eccentric Dr. Pauling and his weird politics have never been taken seriously by American opinion."

This mean-spirited chorus of public disapproval was discouraging to Pauling. And so was the lukewarm praise that Caltech president DuBridge offered via the local newspaper, in which he was quoted saying that "many people have disapproved of some of [Pauling's] methods and activities." There was no word of personal congratulation, no hint of institutional pride, no plan for a grand party of the sort that had followed the announcement of Pauling's chemistry Nobel nine years earlier. There was only, in Pauling's eyes, the unnecessary reminder that "many people have disapproved." He was hurt.

The Peace Prize—and the $50,000 that came with it (about three years' salary for Pauling)—allowed him to do something about it. A few days after reading DuBridge's comment, Pauling called a news conference. As cameras whirred and flashbulbs popped, he announced he was—after more than 40 years as student, faculty member, and head of chemistry—leaving Caltech. He was moving to Santa Barbara, he said, to join the Center for the Study of Democratic Institutions (CSDI), a liberal think tank devoted to studying political and social issues. And very quickly he was gone, first to Norway to accept the Peace Prize, then on to Santa Barbara.

The suddenness of the move caught many of his old friends and coworkers by surprise. Few of them recognized the pressures that had been brought to bear on him because of his political work. Almost no one knew that he had been asked to resign as chairman of the chemistry division. Pauling had kept his humiliation and anger a secret and only now let it out through his decision to leave the place that had been his scientific home.

It was not, as it turned out, the end to Pauling's problems. Santa Barbara was a disappointment. Ava Helen missed her friends in Pasadena. Pauling, intent at first on constructing a new, scientifically based system of ethics, found himself doing little but participating in endless rounds of discussion and debate. "My complaint about the Center," Pauling noted, "is that the great amount of talk leads to little in the way of accepted conclusions."

He also missed doing science. There was no laboratory at CSDI, and without one he could not convince granting agencies in the sciences to give him money for the new ideas he was playing with. Within a few months of his arrival at CSDI, Pauling was thinking about taking a part-time appointment in chemistry at the University of California at Santa Barbara, but the idea was rejected by the university chancellor, who felt Pauling was too controversial.

For the previous decade, Pauling's scientific work had been spotty at best. The research projects he had overseen—most notably a foray into the molecular roots of mental disease and a failed attempt to discover the mechanism of anesthesia—had produced little of value. His only lasting contribution came in 1961, when he and a coworker noted that molecular variations between the hemoglobins from different species could be correlated to the evolutionary distance between them. The more time that had elapsed

Stung by criticism over his political activities from his colleagues at Caltech, Pauling called a news conference on October 18, 1963, to announce that he was ending his relationship with the school to move to a liberal think tank.

since a species separated from another, the greater the difference in the makeup of their hemoglobins. Pauling called this idea a molecular clock and used it to show, for instance, that humans and gorillas may have diverged more recently than was commonly thought. The use of molecular changes to track evolution was an important discovery, one that now—using DNA instead of hemoglobin—constitutes one of the most important tools evolutionary scientists have.

Apart from that, Pauling had little to show. He continued looking for another great idea, one that, like molecular complementarity, would open new vistas of understanding.

In 1965, he found one. Looking for something to read while staying overnight at the house of a psychiatrist friend in Carmel, California, he stumbled across a book describing the use of niacin (one of the B vitamins) in treating a serious mental disease called schizophrenia, in which patients lose touch with reality, behave illogically, and sometimes hear voices. Pauling was struck by the study's finding that using vitamin doses hundreds of times higher than the recommended daily allowance was sometimes successful in treating these cases. He quickly began reading everything he could find on vitamin therapy's effects on brain function.

Within a few weeks, an idea began forming in Pauling's mind. He knew from his reading that the brain is a complex electrochemical system that fires its messages from nerve cell to nerve cell. And from his long experience as a chemist he was aware that chemical reactions work best if there are just the right concentrations of molecules reacting—too little of one or another and the system slows down and does not produce an optimal result. What if the brain were viewed, he wondered, as a large, very complex set of chemical reactions? Optimal mental functioning would result from giving the brain just the right amounts of the needed molecules. In a biological system like the brain, the important molecules would include the enzymes that help reactions happen, the molecules that enzymes work on, and the trace elements, metals, and vitamins needed to help the enzymes do their work. Perhaps, he thought, mental problems resulted from the patient's molecular balance being thrown off kilter. Perhaps the same concept—for which Pauling invented the term *orthomolecular,* to encompass his idea of "the right molecules in the right amounts"—might apply to the rest of the body as well.

This idea was given a boost in 1966. In a New York City speech after receiving the Carl Neuberg Medal, in honor of his work integrating biological and medical science, Pauling mentioned that he hoped he might live another 20 years, to see the great scientific discoveries to come. A few days later he received a letter from Irwin Stone, a biochemist who had been in the audience. Why ask for only 20 years, Stone asked, when you could live another 50 by increasing your intake of vitamin C?

Pauling began corresponding with Stone and learning about vitamin C. He discovered that although vitamin C was a necessary nutrient—without it people die of scurvy—the human body cannot produce it. It has to be taken in through food.

The problem was, Stone was convinced, that the government had decided on a minimum daily requirement for vitamin C that was too low: just enough to prevent scurvy, but not enough to keep the body at peak health. Stone argued that much higher doses of vitamin C could help prevent viral diseases, cancer, and heart disease. How much should humans take? The only good study available of other animals showed that rats, which made their own vitamin C, produced so much that humans would have to ingest 2,000 to 4,000 milligrams (mg) per day to equal it—about 100 times the government's current recommended levels. Stone himself was taking 3,000 mg per day.

Pauling was impressed with Stone's evolutionary argument and began to think that here, too, was another potential example of how providing the ideal rather than the

text continues on page 123

VITAMIN C MUTANTS

If high amounts of vitamin C are so important for health, why don't humans make it themselves? Most animals do, synthesizing their vitamin C internally through a series of enzyme-mediated biochemical reactions. Of all the animals on earth, only a very few—guinea pigs, a fruit-eating bat, a few bird species, and primates, including humans—do not.

The American biochemist Irwin Stone and Linus Pauling believed that humans' inability to make their own vitamin C helped explain not only why they need it in their diet but also why they need so much of it. Twenty-five million years ago, Pauling theorized, a primate ancestor lived in an area where the local fruits and vegetables were particularly rich in vitamin C. In this environment, a mutation eliminating the ability to make vitamin C, perhaps through the loss of a needed enzyme, would not be fatal. There would be enough vitamin C in the diet to make up for it.

In fact, losing the enzyme might actually be advantageous. "These mutant animals would, in the environment that provided an ample supply of ascorbic acid [another name for vitamin C] have an advantage over the ascorbic-acid-producing animals, in that they had been relieved of the burden of constructing and operating the machinery for producing ascorbic acid," Pauling wrote. Freeing the energy formerly needed for making vitamin C would allow the mutant animals to devote that energy to other needs. They would therefore be able to compete more efficiently and would flourish.

In Pauling's view, the system worked well as long as the local diet provided the necessary high levels of vitamin C. But as these primates moved out of their tropical valley, their health began to suffer as their vitamin C intake went down. Their dietary intake of vitamin C was no longer enough to replenish the "natural" levels their bodies had once produced internally.

That, Pauling felt, was why we now needed to supplement our diets with extra doses of vitamin C. It was because we are vitamin C mutants, still trying to regain the health we once enjoyed in that long-ago vitamin C–rich Eden.

text continued from page 121

minimal amounts of a needed molecule might improve health. After doing a little reading on his own and discovering that high doses of vitamin C seemed to pose no significant health dangers, Pauling decided to give it a try. He and Ava Helen both began taking 3,000 mg per day.

The results were astonishing. They each found they had greater energy, an increased sense of well-being, and, best of all, that they seemed to be able to fight off the particularly nasty colds Pauling had long been prone to.

For three years, Pauling kept his ideas about vitamin C and health to himself as he left the CSDI and set about finding a place where he could redevote himself to science. He spent the 1967–68 academic year as a visiting professor at the University of California at San Diego, a position that not only allowed him to teach again but provided him limited laboratory space where he began a series of biochemical experiments with a young, brilliant, hard-working researcher named Art Robinson. The position looked at first as if it might evolve into a permanent one, but a combination of Pauling's age (he was now 67, the standard retirement age for UC professors) and his still-outspoken views on peace (he was now protesting the Vietnam war and sometimes urged students to go on strike to protest American militarism) convinced the university regents to limit their offer to an additional one-year term. Despite his stature as the world's only two-time solo Nobelist, it appeared to them that Pauling was too old and too much trouble to have around.

So he and Ava Helen moved again, this time to Stanford University, where he was able to arrange a position as a consulting professor of chemistry only by agreeing to use his book royalties and investment income to pay half his own salary and all his expenses. Stanford was a great improvement over San Diego, in several ways. For one, the Stanford chemistry faculty and school administrators seemed happy to have Pauling there. For another, there were no problems at this private university with state-mandated retirement ages. And, finally, the location of the school, south of San Francisco in the pleasant, tree-filled small city of Palo Alto, was much closer to a second home the Paulings had built with his Peace Prize money on the spectacular Big Sur coast. Working at Stanford, they could easily travel to Big Sur on weekends and in the summers. After all their wandering, Linus and Ava Helen Pauling settled into the Stanford area for what they hoped would be a very long time.

Art Robinson followed Pauling to Stanford, where he assisted Pauling with new research into the orthomolecular basis of health. Robinson was expert in using gas chromatography, an exquisitely sensitive method of separating and analyzing the chemical components in complex mix-

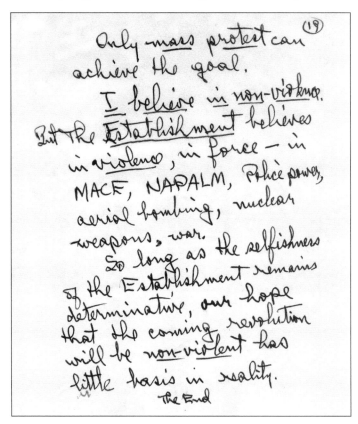

An excerpt from a speech Pauling gave in Los Angeles in 1968 attacking U.S. policy in Vietnam.

tures such as urine and blood, which he combined with computer analysis and used as a tool to track the fate of molecules in the body. Together, Pauling the old theorist and Robinson the young experimentalist were determined to test Pauling's orthomolecular ideas.

Their work went quietly until late 1969, when Pauling, delivering a lecture, noted in passing his success in using vitamin C to prevent colds. Local newspapers spread the story, and soon Pauling's claim that high doses of vitamin C were good for a range of ills became public. In response, several physicians attacked his assertions. Where, they demanded, were the scientific studies needed to prove his ideas?

Pauling began gathering them. He found five well-run, large-scale medical studies that he believed indicated strongly that higher-than-normal doses of vitamin C could reduce the incidence and severity of colds. Some of the studies had provided their subjects with just a little extra vitamin C, and found a small effect. Others had given higher doses and found a greater effect. The largest doses were given in a Swiss study of skiers, where half of a large group got 1,000 mg of extra vitamin C per day and the other half none. The vitamin C group had 61 percent fewer days of upper respiratory illness and a 65 percent decrease in the severity of their colds. It was clear to Pauling that the more vitamin C you took, the healthier you were. This little research exercise convinced Pauling that he was onto something very important. By taking more vitamin C—a cheap, safe nutrient—millions of people could improve their health. The sum of human suffering would decrease. And all this could happen without resorting to expensive physicians or dangerous drugs. Pauling began excitedly writing up his findings for both a scientific journal article and a book for the general public.

It was the beginning of the greatest scientific and public relations roller-coaster ride of Pauling's life. His scientific paper was rejected by *Science*, but his popular book, *Vitamin C and the Common Cold*, published in the fall of 1970, became a best-seller. Pauling promoted his book in newspapers, magazines, radio interviews, and on television. People began buying vitamin C in quantity. Sales double, tripled, and quadrupled over the course of a few months. Drugstores sold out. Manufacturers began building new factories to keep up with the demand. The vitamin industry had never seen anything like it.

But most physicians remained skeptical. The head of the U.S. Food and Drug Administration called the run on vitamin C "ridiculous," saying, "there is no scientific evidence and never have been any meaningful studies indicating that vitamin C is capable of preventing or curing colds." The *Journal of the American Medical Association* said of Pauling's book, "Here are found, not the guarded statements of a philosopher or scientist seeking truths, but the clear, incisive sentences of an advertiser with something to sell. . . . The many admirers of Linus Pauling will wish he had not written this book." Pauling was criticized in the medical press for going directly to the public without first printing his ideas in scientific journals, where submissions were judged by experts before publication; for hand-selecting a few studies that favored his views; and for advocating a significant change in diet without any knowledge of the long-term health effects.

Just as he had done in the nuclear weapons debate, Pauling responded to his critics by fighting harder. He had never argued, he said, that vitamin C could *cure* colds. He understood that humans varied both in their reaction to vitamin C and to colds: Some never got colds whether they took vitamin C or not; others would get colds regardless of how much they took. But for the vast majority, Pauling believed, vitamin C could strengthen the body, increase resistance, prevent some colds, and lessen the effects of others. He then challenged his critics to bring forward one case where a few grams a day of pure vitamin C had harmed anyone (beyond an occasional bout of diarrhea or a stomach upset, they could not). And he continued finding more medical studies to back up his views.

He also pointed out that he had tried to go through the scientific press and been turned down. But being turned down did not deter him. He believed the public had a right to know about this chance to improve their health, so he had gone directly to them. As for his critics in the medical press, didn't the medical press make quite a bit of money off of cold remedy advertisers?

People began taking sides in the great vitamin C debate. On one side were most physicians, some nutrition-ists, and a few other scientists who said Pauling was an old Nobelist who was far out of his field, a nutritional quack, a health faddist, a kook. On the other were a few scientists who knew Pauling well enough to treat his insights with respect—and 50 million people who, by the mid-1970s, were all taking extra daily doses of vitamin C.

The administrators of Stanford University were not happy to see one of their faculty members being called a quack. Nor were they pleased with Pauling's repeated calls to students to protest the Vietnam War. It was thus not a great surprise when, in the early 1970s, they turned down Pauling and Robinson's request for more room to conduct vitamin C studies.

Robinson came up with a solution. He knew a wealthy manufacturer of gas chromatography equipment who would provide them money for laboratory space off cam-pus. Why not quit Stanford and start their own research institute? They could have their own scientific home, raise their own money, and be their own bosses.

Pauling agreed to give it a try. In the spring of 1973 an arrangement was made for funding, and he and Robinson announced that they were going to open the new Institute of Orthomolecular Medicine a few miles away from Stanford.

Now 72 years old, Pauling threw himself into the new venture with the energy of a young man. While Robinson set up the complicated laboratory equipment and oversaw the day-to-day management of the institute, Pauling began traveling, speaking, and writing grant requests to raise the money needed to fund new research projects into the health benefits of vitamin C. The more he learned, the more convinced he became that increased vitamin C was beneficial not only for colds, but for preventing the flu, for extending the average lifespan—even for treating cancer.

But he had a difficult time convincing any granting agency to help him prove his ideas. The National Cancer Institute turned down his grant requests, saying that the existing evidence was too sketchy and Pauling's institute too small to support major studies. Unable to raise money from the usual sources, Pauling turned to the public. The power of his name had convinced millions of Americans to take extra vitamin C, and now the power of his name was added to appeals to the public to help support his institute, which was renamed The Linus Pauling Institute of Science and Medicine. A professional fundraiser was hired and a huge campaign of advertisements and direct mail requests for contributions begun.

The public responded. Hundreds of thousands of dollars began to flow into the institute in the mid-1970s. Robinson began dreaming of relocating to Oregon, building a brand-new institute and expanding to become an internationally respected research center.

This dream was not shared by others at the institute. Many of the researchers and employees liked it in California and did not want to move. And some were unhappy as well with Robinson's sometimes authoritarian management style. Instead of making great research possible, the money broke the Pauling institute into warring camps.

Robinson was on one side, Pauling the other. Robinson had given up his career at San Diego to follow Pauling and was now staking his entire future on the institute. While Pauling continued traveling widely to speak on peace issues and spent a good deal of his time secluded at his Big Sur ranch, Robinson spent every minute keeping the place going. He had his own ideas about vitamin C as well, and began redirecting experiments to fit those theories. "Art had gotten into the habit of thinking of the institute as his institute," Pauling later said.

But it was not Robinson's institute—it was Pauling's. And when Pauling heard about the staff dissatisfaction, and at the same time learned that Robinson had begun turning the vitamin C research into areas that he had not agreed to, he decided enough was enough. In June 1978, he asked Robinson to resign. Robinson refused to do that. Instead, outraged at the way he had been treated, he sued Linus Pauling and the institute for $25.5 million.

This was enough bad news, but there was worse to come. Ava Helen fell ill, and the diagnosis was bad: cancer of the stomach. The resulting surgery weakened her tremendously. She seemed to age 10 years in a few months.

Linus and Ava Helen a few years before her death in 1981.

But despite her physician's recommendation, she would not take chemotherapy. Instead, she increased her intake of vitamin C to 10,000 mg per day.

For a while, it seemed to work. She regained her energy and strength, and felt well enough to accompany Pauling on his many speaking trips. She took up music, learning to play folk songs on the guitar and buying a grand piano for their Big Sur home. She and Pauling were inseparable during those times in the late 1970s. They were good days, full of love and music, visits from her children and grandchildren and, best of all, the weeks when Linus and she were alone, just the two of them, old lovers listening to the sea.

In 1981, however, the cancer came back. This time no amount of vitamin C could help her, although Pauling kept trying. He still held on to the hope that massive doses would perform a miracle, as it had with some patients with advanced cancer that had been reported in Scotland, that somehow he could make her cancer disappear. He worked ceaselessly to save her.

But this was one battle he could not win. Ava Helen died at home on December 7, 1981.

The first few months after her death were the hardest. Pauling found himself moaning uncontrollably and wept whenever her name was mentioned. He would never fully stop grieving. Slowly, however, he learned how to get on with his life alone.

Because of Pauling's urging, the National Cancer Institute had decided to fund a pair of studies at the internationally respected Mayo Clinic in Minnesota to see if vitamin C really could help cancer patients. Pauling had eagerly awaited the results but was deeply disappointed when they were published. Both studies of terminal cancer patients appeared to show that the vitamin had no effect in prolonging life. The medical community took this as the final word on the subject, although Pauling spent months trying to convince them the studies were flawed.

In 1986, he published a book of health advice titled *How to Live Longer and Feel Better*, which distilled everything he had learned about vitamins, minerals, and diet. The cover was graced with a picture of Pauling in his mid-80s, still vibrant, ruddy, bright-eyed, and evidently glowing with good health, a walking advertisement for vitamin C. The book was another best-seller.

Even in his mid-80s, and without Ava Helen, Pauling continued to travel extensively, speak widely, and publish regularly on topics from crystal structure to nuclear physics, superconductivity to human metabolism, chemical bonding to world peace. He never stopped receiving awards and honorary doctorates, or advocating vitamin C.

Then, slowly, much more so than he had once hoped, scientific opinion began shifting his way. A new group of younger researchers began looking at vitamin C from a new angle, studying its abilities as an antioxidant, a substance that stops destructive bits of molecular debris called free radicals from damaging cells. In 1990, the National Cancer Institute, impressed by the growing body of evidence, sponsored an international conference on vitamin C. There were presentations on the vitamin's importance in metabolic reactions, its effect in delaying tumor onset and growth, and its ability to prolong survival times, reduce treatment toxicity, and increase the efficacy of other treatments. "It was great! A great affair!" Pauling said when it was over.

And the evidence kept mounting. A medical newsletter pointed to the fact that vitamin C had been shown to have a protective effect against various cancers in 34 of 47 studies examined. *Time* magazine ran a cover story about amazing benefits apparently attributable to taking extra vitamins, especially antioxidants such as vitamin C. An epidemiological study showed that men who took an extra 500 mg of C per day could expect to live an average of five years longer than men who did not. In 1992, at the end of a special meeting of the New York Academy of Sciences devoted to

Linus Pauling in the study of his Big Sur home in 1987. He spent his final years overseeing health research at his institute and trying to describe the structure of atomic nuclei.

studies of high-dose vitamins and other nutrients, a nutrition professor rose and said, "For three days I have been listening to talks about the value of large intakes of vitamin C and other natural substances, and I have not heard a single mention of the name Linus Pauling. Has not the time come when we should admit that Linus Pauling was right all along?" The response was a prolonged round of enthusiastic applause.

Pauling, now in his 90s, was pleased by the good news, but he no longer cared as much as he once might have. He himself had been diagnosed with cancer. He underwent a series of surgeries in the winter of 1991–92, then began treating himself with high doses of vitamin C, raw fruits and vegetables, and an experimental technique to boost his immune system.

He spent most of his time at the Big Sur ranch, perched on the edge of a bluff over the Pacific, making calculations, entertaining old friends who came to visit, looking out to sea. His children took turns taking care of him. He completed a final set of papers on the structure of atomic nuclei, a subject that had interested him since his early student days at Caltech. Then he laid down his pen.

Linus Pauling died at Big Sur on August 19, 1994.

CHRONOLOGY

1901
Linus Carl Pauling born February 28 in Portland, Oregon

1917
Enters Oregon Agricultural College's (OAC's) program in chemical engineering

1919–20
Serves a year as an instructor in chemistry at OAC

1922
Begins graduate work in physical chemistry at the California Institute of Technology (Caltech)

1923
Marries Ava Helen Miller on June 17

1925
Earns his doctorate at Caltech; first child, Linus, Jr., born March 10

1926–27
Spends 19 months on a Guggenheim Fellowship studying quantum physics in Europe

1927
Appointed assistant professor of theoretical chemistry at Caltech

1929
Publishes his principles for determining the structures of complex crystals

1930–35
Focuses his work on explaining the nature of the chemical bond in terms of the new quantum mechanics

1931
Appointed full professor at Caltech; publishes first paper in the influential "Nature of the Chemical Bond" series; wins the A. C. Langmuir Prize as the best young chemist in the nation; second son, Peter, is born on February 10

1932
Daughter Linda is born May 31

1933
Becomes the youngest person elected to the National Academy of Sciences

1934–1940
Begins work on the structure of proteins, including important research on hemoglobin, protein denaturation, and hydrogen bonding

1937
Named chairman of the Caltech Division of Chemistry and Chemical Engineering; fourth child, Edward Crellin, born June 4

1939
Publishes *The Nature of the Chemical Bond, and The Structure of Molecules and Crystals*, one of the most-cited scientific texts of the century

1940
Publishes his theory of the structure and formation of antibodies

1941–45
After recovering from a battle with a life-threatening kidney disease, devotes himself to war research on rocket propellants and explosives, artificial plasma and artificial antibodies, and invents an oxygen-measuring device for use in submarines

1946
Joins the Emergency Committee of Atomic Scientists, and begins 15 years of anti-bomb activism

1947
Publishes *General Chemistry*, an influential and profitable college textbook

1948
Spends six months in England as the Eastman Professor at Oxford University

1949

Serves as president of the American Chemical Society; publishes, with Harvey Itano and John Singer, an influential paper on the molecular basis of sickle-cell anemia

1950–52

With his assistant Robert Corey, outlines in precise detail the basic structural features of a number of proteins

1952

Because of his anti-bomb activism, Pauling is labeled a Communist and denied a passport to travel outside the United States

1952–53

Works on and publishes an incorrect structure for DNA

1954

Wins the Nobel Prize in Chemistry for his work on the chemical bond and the structure of complex molecules

1956–61

Works on the molecular basis of brain function and a theory of anesthesia. Continues his political activism, speaking widely about the dangers of radioactive fallout from bomb tests and the need for world peace

1958

Publishes *No More War!;* and with his wife, Ava Helen, presents to the Secretary-General of the United Nations a petition to end nuclear testing signed by more than 11,000 scientists worldwide; is forced to resign as head of the chemistry division at Caltech in part because of the negative reaction among trustees and donors to his peace work

1960

Refuses to provide a subcommittee of the U.S. Senate the names of those who helped him circulate his anti-testing petition

1963

On the day the world's first nuclear test-ban treaty goes into effect, Pauling is awarded the 1962 Nobel Peace Prize

1963–67
Joins the Center for the Study of Democratic Institutions in Santa Barbara, California

1966
First becomes interested in the use of large doses of vitamin C to prevent disease

1967–69
Research professor at the University of California, San Diego

1969–72
Professor of Chemistry at Stanford University

1970
Publishes *Vitamin C and the Common Cold,* which convinces tens of thousands of people to take more vitamin C

1973
Founds, with Arthur Robinson, his own research institute devoted to health issues, including the effects of vitamin C

1979
Publishes, with Ewan Cameron, *Vitamin C and Cancer*

1981
Ava Helen Pauling dies of stomach cancer

1986
Publishes *How to Live Longer and Feel Better*

1991
Pauling diagnosed with rectal and prostate cancer

1994
Linus Pauling dies on August 19

FURTHER READING

Books and Articles by Linus Pauling

Marinacci, Barbara, ed. *Linus Pauling in His Own Words.* New York: Simon & Schuster, 1995.

Pauling, Linus. *The Nature of the Chemical Bond and the Structure of Molecules and Crystals.* Ithaca, N.Y.: Cornell University Press, 1939.

——. *No More War!* New York: Dodd, Mead, 1958.

——. *Linus Pauling on Science and Peace.* New York: Fund for the Republic, 1964.

——. *General Chemistry,* 3d ed. San Francisco: Freeman, 1970.

——. "Fifty Years of Progress in Structural Chemistry and Molecular Biology." *Daedalus,* Fall 1970, pp. 988–1014.

——. *Vitamin C and the Common Cold.* 2d ed. New York: Bantam Books, 1971.

——. *How to Live Longer and Feel Better.* New York: Freeman, 1986.

Pauling, Linus, and Roger Hayward. *The Architecture of Molecules.* San Francisco: W. H. Freeman, 1964.

Books and Articles about Linus Pauling

Collier, Peter. "The Old Man and the C." *New West,* April 24, 1978, pp. 21–25.

Goertzel, Ted, and Ben Goertzel. *Linus Pauling: A Life in Science and Politics.* New York: Basic Books, 1995.

Hager, Thomas. *Force of Nature: The Life of Linus Pauling.* New York: Simon & Schuster, 1995.

Horgan, John. "Profile: Linus C. Pauling—Stubbornly Ahead of His Time." *Scientific American,* March 1993, pp. 36–37.

Ikeda, Daisaku. *A Lifelong Quest for Peace: A Dialogue Between Linus Pauling and Daisaku Ikeda.* Boston: Jones and Bartlett, 1992.

Servos, John. *Physical Chemistry from Ostwald to Pauling.* Princeton, N.J.: Princeton University Press, 1990.

White, Florence Meiman. *Linus Pauling: Scientist and Crusader.* New York: Walker, 1980.

Books about Pauling's Scientific Interests

Asimov, Isaac. *Asimov's Biographical Encyclopedia of Science and Technology.* 2d ed. Garden City, N.Y.: Doubleday, 1982.

Brock, William H. *The Norton History of Chemistry.* New York: Norton, 1993.

Crick, Francis. *What Mad Pursuit.* New York: Basic Books, 1988.

Edelstein, Stuart J. *The Sickled Cell: From Myth to Molecules.* Cambridge: Harvard University Press, 1986.

Fruton, Joseph. *Molecules and Life.* New York: Wiley, 1972.

Goodstein, Judith R. *Millikan's School.* New York: Norton, 1991.

Huemer, Richard P., ed. *The Roots of Molecular Medicine: A Tribute to Linus Pauling.* New York: Freeman, 1986.

James, Laylin, ed. *Nobel Laureates in Chemistry, 1901-1992.* Washington, D.C.: American Chemical Society and the Chemical Heritage Foundation, 1993.

Judson, Horace Freeland. *The Eighth Day of Creation: The Makers of the Revolution in Biology.* New York: Simon & Schuster, 1980.

Kay, Lily. *The Molecular Vision of Life.* New York: Oxford University Press, 1993.

Kendrew, John. *The Thread of Life.* Cambridge, Mass.: Harvard University Press, 1966.

Kevles, Daniel J. *The Physicists.* Cambridge, Mass.: Harvard University Press, 1987.

Olby, Robert. *The Path to the Double Helix.* Seattle: University of Washington Press, 1974.

Rich, Alexander, and Norman Davidson, eds. *Structural Chemistry and Molecular Biology.* San Francisco: Freeman, 1968.

Richards, Evelleen. *Vitamin C and Cancer: Medicine or Politics?* New York: St. Martin's, 1991.

Silverstein, Arthur M. *A History of Immunology.* San Diego: Academic Press, 1989.

Watson, James D. *The Double Helix: A Personal Account of the Discovery and Structure of DNA.* New York: Atheneum, 1968.

Wolf, Fred Alan. *Taking the Quantum Leap.* San Francisco: Harper & Row, 1981.

Zuckerman, Harriet. *The Scientific Elite.* New York: Free Press, 1977.

Books about Pauling's Political Interests

Bernal, J. D. *The Social Function of Science.* New York: Macmillan, 1939.

Caute, David. *The Great Fear.* New York: Simon & Schuster, 1978.

Divine, Robert A. *Blowing on the Wind.* New York: Oxford University Press, 1978.

Kamen, Martin D. *Radiant Science, Dark Politics.* Berkeley: University of California Press, 1985.

Smith, Alice Kimball. *A Peril and a Hope: The Scientists' Movement in America 1945–47.* Chicago: University of Chicago Press, 1965.

Tom Hager is a science writer and Director of Special Projects at the University of Oregon. He has written two other books, including *Force of Nature: The Life of Linus Pauling* and scores of magazine articles about science and health. He lives in Eugene, Oregon, with his wife, Lauren Kessler, and their children, Jackson, Zane, and Elizabeth.

Owen Gingerich is Professor of Astronomy and of the History of Science at the Harvard-Smithsonian Center for Astrophysics in Cambridge, Massachusetts. The author of more than 400 articles and reviews, he has also written *The Great Copernicus Chase and Other Adventures in Astronomical History* and *The Eye of Heaven: Ptolemy, Copernicus, Kepler.*